THE GREAT TIT

HAMLYN SPECIES GUIDES

THE GREAT TIT

Andrew Gosler

HAMLYN

To Caroline and Chris, for the time to watch and write.

First published in 1993 by Hamlyn Limited,
an imprint of Reed Consumer Books Limited
Michelin House, 81 Fulham Road, London SW3 6RB
and Auckland, Melbourne, Singapore and Toronto

Copyright © Reed International Books Limited 1993

Text copyright © Andrew Gosler 1993
Illustrations copyright © Norman Arlott 1993
Map copyright © Reed International Books Limited 1993
Photographs copyright © Andrew Gosler, except for page 110 copyright © C.M. Perrins.

ISBN 0 600 57950 6

A CIP catalogue record for this book is available from the British Library

Page design by Jessica Caws
Maps by Louise Griffiths
Printed in Hong Kong

COVER ILLUSTRATION *A male Great Tit presents a caterpillar to his mate in response to
her wing shivering display and distinctive 'zeedling' call. This extra food is essential
to allow her to develop eggs.*

CONTENTS

Series Editor's Foreword

THE Great Tit has the widest distribution of all the tit species, extending from the Atlantic seaboard right across Europe and Asia to the Pacific coast, and ranging from the Arctic conditions of north Scandinavia to tropical mangroves of Malaysia. In many areas, and especially in Britain, it is a familiar bird. We see it in our gardens, where it may nest in special nestboxes or where it visits in winter to take the food that we put out. We hear its familiar 'tea-cher tea-cher' song in a local park or woodland, marvelling that this relatively small bird will sing even in the middle of winter. Its attractively coloured plumage, with black-and-white head pattern and with yellow underparts divided by a striking black belly-stripe, cannot fail to impress.

As it so readily takes to nestboxes, and is easy to see and hear in gardens, parks and woodland, it is not surprising that this species has been the subject of a phenomenal volume of scientific studies of its nesting behaviour, feeding habits and various other aspects of its biology. Yet surely the majority of us know comparatively little about the true life of the Great Tit, apart perhaps from the fact that, like other tits, it lays a large number of eggs. Even that trait, however, is not so simple as it may seem – for the number of eggs a female Great Tit lays depends on several factors, including, for example, time of year, the year itself, the particular habitat, weather conditions and food supply (or anticipated food supply), and on the individual female herself.

This sprightly and cheerful creature holds many secrets and surprises for the enquiring mind of an ornithologist or bird-lover. While reading Dr Gosler's fascinating text, much of it the result of his own extensive field studies and research, I have learned a great deal about the Great Tit's methods of seeking and finding food, about its population dynamics and the factors that determine which young birds are recruited into the breeding population – and a lot more besides.

Despite all the research, however, there remains much to be discovered. Very little is known, for instance, about the Great Tit's general biology and behaviour over most of its non-European range. What better way to understand how to embark on the route to discovery than to read and reflect on the chapters presented here.

David Christie

An adult male Great Tit monopolizes a peanut feeder. Social status often detemines access to food in Great Tit society.

Preface

'It is hardly necessary to give any detailed description of the life and habits of so familiar a bird.' T. Gompertz (1961)

'. . . so much has been published on the European tits that it is difficult to synthesize it now.' C. M. Perrins (1979)

'The Great Tit is perhaps the most-studied small bird in the world.'
R. H. McCleery and C. M. Perrins (1988)

THE statements above all refer to (or largely to) the Great Tit, and each one introduced a major contribution to the literature on the species, but they share another, and rather curious, feature. Behind each, there seemed to be an apology for having added to that massive literature – for it is massive. Since 1979 alone (the year in which Christopher Perrins published his important work *British Tits*), some seven hundred scientific papers have been published which present information on this species. Perhaps the most paradoxical of the extracts is that of Gompertz. This is not only because, contrary to her argument, familiarity more often breeds contempt for, rather than a fuller understanding of, a bird's biology, but also because the sentence introduced a 49-page paper on the vocabulary of the Great Tit.

Why do ornithologists feel the need to apologize for studying this bird? I suspect that there are two reasons. The first is a general issue that I shall not dwell on here. Through the study of birds, ornithologists have made an enormous contribution to the fields of animal behaviour, ecology and evolutionary biology. Despite this, in the cutthroat rough and tumble of professional science it is still unfashionable to describe oneself as an ornithologist. This is because, traditionally, ornithologists are often thought to study birds because they find them compelling and fascinating in their own right rather than because they offer some greater insight into the larger and 'more important' questions in biology upon which ornithology can shed light. Hence, in their desire to throw off this mantle of subjectivity and to compete convincingly for research grants and publication space, ornithologists constantly feel obliged to present objective reasons for their work. This is reflected to some extent in at least one of the extracts above.

The second reason for apology is related to the first, but is more specific to the Great Tit. It stems from the assumption that, after some sixty years of intensive study, we must know everything that we could possibly want to know about the Great Tit, and so our efforts might be better engaged elsewhere. Indeed, ornithologists working in this area are often challenged with such sentiments by both lay people and other ornithologists. Such impressions have developed in a social and political climate in which scientists are required increasingly to justify the search for knowledge itself. This view, however, is naïve for three reasons. First, quite simply because the Great Tit has proved to be a near-ideal subject through which to examine questions in ecology and evolutionary biology, so providing the objective direction and scientific credibility sought by ornithologists generally (see above). In many cases, these are questions which have an important bearing on the conservation of wild-bird populations: for example, by trying to understand the underlying mechanisms of population dynamics we hope to be able to predict the effects of our own activities on bird numbers. Second, the view is naïve because it fails to recognize the nature of biological research. The complexity of the processes being examined means that every 'answer' generates more questions. For example, it has long been known that changes in Great Tit populations from year to year are due largely to differences in juvenile mortality between years and that this was in some way related to the abundance of tree seeds in winter, but the discovery that mortality occurred largely before the young birds were feeding on those seeds in autumn showed that the relationship was not nearly so simple. Many of the fundamental questions of bird ecology have taken decades to answer, because we have needed to track populations over many years before we could examine the causes of changes in those populations. For example, it is only in recent years that any real understanding of some of the relationships between the breeding biology of the tits and the abundance of their caterpillar prey has been achieved. Some issues have been impossible to tackle until recently, because we lacked the methods or technology to broach them. Hence, discussion of the genetics of Great Tit populations was virtually unknown before 1980 and was utterly theoretical before 1970. Third, it is naïve because the most important resource of the biologist is ideas, and there is not a finite supply of these. We cannot ignore the opportunity which the Great Tit gives us to test new ideas in ecology, behavioural ecology or evolutionary biology. Nor can we ignore the opportunities afforded by the development of new methodology or technology to re-examine old ideas. This is necessary because cases are rarely proven beyond doubt in this science. Rather, evidence is sought through the balance of probability.

So, why is the Great Tit so attractive to ecologists and evolutionary biologists? There are many reasons. It is a comparatively common bird throughout much of its range, but especially in Western Europe, where the biologists live. It occurs in a number of different habitat types. It is one of a group of closely related species, several of which are often found at a single site. Furthermore, these species are resident across much of their range in Europe. Like its relatives, the Great Tit is sociable outside the breeding season, and forms single- or mixed-species feeding flocks. During the breeding season it is generally territorial, a fact which it proclaims by a distinctive but varied song. It has an extremely broad diet, which differs between individuals and seasons. It is easily attracted to food provided by man. It is an important predator of insects (including many pest species), especially during the breeding season, but itself falls prey to several other animals. It has large families. Perhaps most importantly for the biologist, however, it is a hole-nester which readily accepts artificial nestboxes in which to breed, and often also in which to roost. Indeed, perhaps the only drawback of this bird is that, although not difficult to keep, it has proved difficult to breed in captivity. The significance for the ornithologist of each of these facets of the Great Tit's biology will become clear as the book develops. For now, it is enlightening to consider just the bird's use of nestboxes, and perhaps a little irony in the history of science.

The first recorded use of nestboxes provided for passerines dates from the late Middle Ages. These were set up to attract sparrows and Starlings for food. In the nineteenth century, wooden boxes began to be provided by naturalists. The large-scale provision of boxes, however, dates only from the early twentieth century. For example, in 1905, the Baron von Berlepsch had some 2300 boxes on his estates in Germany. These were extremely successful, and it is said that over 90 per cent of them were occupied. Most of these boxes were provided in forests in the hope of increasing the numbers of insectivorous birds. These were thought to be beneficial, as it was assumed that they would exert some control on the trees' insect pests. Without data to contradict this, such beliefs were widespread in those early days of ecology. For example, a leaflet entitled simply 'Titmice (Paridae)', published by the British Board of Agriculture and Fisheries in 1913, implored foresters and fruit-growers to encourage tits to breed on their estates because of their beneficial feeding habits, and especially '...the Great Tit, which is a voracious devourer of insects of all kinds and in all stages'. Here lies the irony, for, although interest in nestbox populations of tits has developed steadily over the last century, there is little evidence that the depredations of these birds impose much control on pest numbers (Speight and Wainhouse 1989), although we shall see later that the impression that they make on the abundance of their caterpillar prey cannot be entirely insignificant. There is a further irony to which I shall return shortly.

The first serious study of a Great Tit population (that is to say one in which the numbers of pairs using the boxes and details of their breeding were monitored) was started near Wageningen in the Netherlands by K. Wolda in 1912. Pest control was one of the driving forces behind that study. Wolda published few of the data from this study, but in 1936 H.N. Kluijver became involved with the project and began to ring the nestlings in the boxes each year. Since it was now possible to identify each bird individually by its unique ring number, the possibility arose of studying the number of birds in the population in terms of the four processes which determine it: births (natality), deaths (mortality), and movements into (immigration) and out from (emigration) the population. In reality, it is often difficult to distinguish between emigration and mortality, as we shall see, but it is only by recognizing birds as individuals that we can even come close to attempting it. The Dutch study, carried out by members of the Institute of Ecological Research (now the Netherlands Institute for Ecology), continues to this day. Studies have been made at a number of sites, including Liesbosch and Oosterhout, but chiefly at the Hoge Veluwe near Arnhem and on the Friesian island of Vlieland. This latter site has been particularly useful for looking at population processes and genetics, because the population there suffers low rates of immigration and emigration.

Incubation of the clutch can take up to four hundred hours for the Great Tit.
This duty is undertaken entirely by the female although the male feeds her several
times each hour.

In 1951, Kluijver published a seminal paper in the Dutch journal *Ardea* on his results. This has had considerable influence in ornithology and ecology generally. Kluijver's studies had, however, been noticed before then. Between 1947 and 1950, strongly influenced by the Dutch study, David Lack (director of the Edward Grey Institute of Field Ornithology at Oxford University), together with John Gibb, set up two hundred nestboxes in the 27 ha (67 acres) of Marley Wood and the Oxford University estate at Wytham. In the late 1950s and early 1960s, Christopher Perrins expanded this study to cover the Wytham Woods estate, so today there are some 960 boxes in 320 ha of woodland. In 1989, Roger Riddington and I expanded the study again by adding 165 boxes in gardens, hedgerows and small copses in the vicinity of Wytham to look at movements in and out of Wytham and study breeding success and body condition of the birds in a range of habitats.

While the Dutch and British projects are the longest running, several important studies of other populations have now been undertaken for more than twenty years. These include sites in Belgium, Germany, Sweden and

Finland, and more recently nestbox studies have been established in France, Switzerland, Spain, Hungary, Italy and Israel. Shorter studies have also been made in Japan. Reference to many of these will be made at appropriate times in the text, but inevitably there will be a bias towards the British and Dutch work. While population studies have motivated much of the work on the Great Tit, the species has also proved an ideal subject for the behavioural ecologist. Hence, detailed studies of territoriality, foraging behaviour, song and visual communication, including both field and laboratory work, have been carried out in many of these study populations. In many respects, the attributes which make the Great Tit a suitable candidate for population research also make it attractive for behavioural research, and data for both sorts of study can be collected simultaneously. For example, in asking why Great Tits sing the number of songs that they do, workers have looked at the repertoires of known individuals and tried to relate the number in each to aspects of the singer's fitness, such as longevity and breeding success.

In this preface, I have presented forceful reasons why scientists continue to study the Great Tit. There can, however, be dangers in taking too hard-nosed and objective an attitude to one's research while hoping to avoid a label of 'ornithologist'. For one thing, it has led to some curious statements in the literature as to why the Great Tit is the subject of so much interest. Too often have I read that the Great Tit is a *typical* small woodland passerine. It is not. In most of the communities in which it is found, it is one of the larger of the 'small' passerines present. In this respect it is not even typical of its genus, since in most communities it is at least a third larger than its next largest relative. This means that it tends to be socially dominant over other tits, and this is not typical. Nor is its extensive geographical range typical of its genus. The large families which it raises are typical only of tits and of nuthatches, which are closely related; most woodland passerines lay only four to six eggs, rather than the eight or more laid by these birds. Even in its hole-nesting it is rather atypical, since its large size excludes it from using many holes which are available to smaller species. Its larger size also influences its foraging behaviour, so that in winter it feeds on the ground far more than any of its relatives. The simple fact is that the Great Tit is convenient. Inevitably, the huge literature on this species makes it a model with which other species will be compared. It is, however, a model which we have produced because we have chosen to work on it, and not because it represents some kind of avian 'Mr Average' from which other species deviate. The Great Tit is as much adapted to a particular ecology as is any other species, although it may be more flexible in its behaviour than many others.

I hinted earlier that there was a further irony in the history of work on the Great Tit. This is related to the fact that the principal feature which makes it convenient for research lies in its ready acceptance of nestboxes. It has been difficult to explain certain results in the ecological and evolutionary studies made on these populations. These are results which appear consistently in different populations and I shall describe them later in the book. We now know that there are several ways in which the provision of nestboxes may alter the characteristics of a population. These may result from a surplus of suitable nest sites or a reduction in the rates of predation or parasite infestation. Hence, it has recently been suggested that the great edifice of knowledge on this species might be built on shaky foundations (Møller 1989, 1992). There are strong arguments against this point of view which will be considered later, but the very suggestion serves to emphasize that it is chiefly the Great Tit's convenience as a subject that has attracted biologists for so many years.

In this book I hope to show that, whatever our motivation for research, the Great Tit is a fascinating creature which, in its own right, deserves the attention that it receives. We have been fortunate that its behaviour and ecology have allowed us to look a little more deeply into the life of this bird than into the lives of many others. Its biology has proved to be far more complex than ever could have been anticipated fifty years ago. What we have discovered, and continue to discover, about it should not simply act as a model for comparison, but rather the intricacy of its life should inspire work on other species which lend themselves less readily to study. After all, the Great Tit is no more nor less interesting than any other species. In this, at least, it is typical. It would be a sorry situation indeed if, as ornithologists, we could not wonder a little at the life history of any bird, but had only to observe them with objective indifference as we sought the general principles of biological theory. Certainly we need make no apology.

A.G.G.
Oxford 1992

Acknowledgements

No book was ever written without the support of others and so I should like to record my gratitude to those who have assisted me during the production of this. I thank Jo Hemmings at Hamlyn for the invitation to write the book in the first place, and Jo, Cathy Lowne and Louise Dick for their skill, advice and encouragement throughout the project. If this book is a success, it is in no small measure to Norman Arlott's splendid contribution. I thank David Christie for the surgical precision with which he has wielded the editor's pen. I am especially grateful to Professors Christopher Perrins and John Krebs for commenting constructively on the text: I have also benefited enormously from their guidance. Finally, for her valuable criticism of the whole text and for her constant support, I thank my wife, Caroline Jackson-Houlston.

1

THE GREAT TIT

THE Great Tit is one of the most familiar birds in Western Europe. Its wide distribution, distinctive plumage, affinity for human habitation and almost ceaseless vocalization mean that it rarely escapes notice. However, although our encounters with it may seem commonplace, we should be mistaken if we thought that its life (or the life of any bird) was uninteresting. Research carried out over the last sixty years has shown that the Great Tit interacts with its environment in ways far more complex than imagined when these studies began. Furthermore, there is still a great deal that is not fully understood. I shall explore some of the aspects of the Great Tit's life that have drawn the attention of ornithologists for more than two generations. Indeed, so great has been the attention paid to this bird that it is widely held to be the most studied species in the world. In the preface I suggested some of the reasons for this intense interest. In this chapter and the next, I shall present an overview of the species. I hope that the significance of at least some of these reasons will become more apparent.

The tit family

Although the Great Tit is a small passerine, weighing 13–21 g (½–¾ oz), it is one of the largest of the 53 species of parine (subfamily Parinae) or true tits. With the subfamily Remizinae (twelve species of penduline tit), the Parinae make up the Paridae: tits and chickadees (Sibley and Monroe 1990). There are parine tits in the Palearctic (Eurasia), Oriental, Nearctic (North America) and Ethiopian (sub-Saharan Africa) zoogeographical regions, but few in the Neotropical (Central and South America) and Australasian regions. However, the subfamily's diversity is concentrated in the Old World, with 29 species on the Eurasian landmass. Of these, only the Siberian Tit is also found in North America, although ten species are solely found there. None of them occurs in sub-Saharan Africa, where fourteen more species occur exclusively.

Most (51) parine species are grouped within a single genus: *Parus*. The remainder comprise two further genera, restricted to south-east Asia. The *Parus* species are highly active, acrobatic birds, found in terrestrial habitats with trees or shrubs. They have short, strong bills, strong feet, rounded wings of medium length and a medium, square-ended tail. They vary in colour, but most are of browns and greys. Yellows, blues and greens are found more

The nominate race of the Great Tit. The adult male is generally brighter than the female, and in the width of his belly-stripe. In many populations he is also some 4 per cent larger than she is. The juvenile is generally duller than the adults, and has green wing coverts and yellow cheeks.

Parus major major
(adult male)

Parus major major
(adult female)

Parus major major
(juvenile)

Norman Arlott

commonly in the Old World tits. Many of the species are boldly marked, often with contrasting black or white against yellows, greens or browns. The upperparts are usually of a more or less uniform brown or green; the under-parts are generally uniform also, but paler or of yellow or white. Unlike many other passerine groups such as larks or buntings, the tits lack streaking, spotting or banding in their plumage. Nevertheless, various species show many other plumage marks such as wingbars, belly-stripes, and contrasting outer tail feathers. A recurring pattern is a darker crown or cap with con-trasting paler cheeks, often set off against a dark bib which may be small, as in the Blue Tit, or large, as in the Sombre Tit (page 43). Some species also show eye-stripes and supercilia, as in the Mountain Chickadee (page 102).

Most of the nine *Parus* species in the Western Palearctic (essentially Europe) extend their ranges into the Eastern Palearctic (page 43). Only the Blue and Sombre Tits are more or less restricted to the Western Palearctic. Six Palearctic species occur also in the Oriental region, and six more species are restricted to the latter area. The Great Tit is the only *Parus* to extend its range across the Western and the Eastern Palearctic, and into the Oriental region. Its present distribution and racial differentiation reflect a complex history of range extension and retreat and of temporary geographic iso-lation, which forms an interesting biosystematic case study in its own right.

Form and variation

Since its formal description by Carl von Linné (Linnaeus) in 1758, more than sixty geographic races or subspecies of the Great Tit have been described on the basis of plumage and distribution. Many of these are now thought to be erroneous, and I shall follow the comprehensive revisions of Delacour and Vaurie (1950), Snow (1953) and Vaurie (1959), and recognize thirty sub-species. While each of these is defined by its range and some combination of colour, size or morphology (such as bill shape), for convenience they are most easily considered as forming four groups or allospecies (*major, minor, cinereus* and *bokharensis*, but *see bokharensis* on page 20) shown on page 23 with ranges overleaf. The basic pattern is of a strong black bill, black lore, cap, nape and collar, chin, throat and belly-stripe contrasted against white cheeks, pale underparts and darker upperparts and tail, with a white wedge formed by the outer tail feathers, although the extent of this varies greatly among races and is virtually absent in a few. The junction of the black nape with the mantle is marked by a pale (often yellowish) nuchal spot, and the wing shows a yellow, cream or white wingbar formed by con-trasting tips to the greater secondary coverts. The legs are blue-grey.

The variation in size indicated by the weight range has many sources. In many populations, males are 4 per cent larger than females (reflected in wing and tarsus length). In an area, birds may vary in size between habitats as a result of differences in nutrition during their development as nestlings. Most variation, however, results from geographic differences. Snow (1954) showed that, in each of three main divisions of the species, body size declined as the mean temperature of the coldest month increased: that is, the birds in warmer areas tended to be smaller. This follows a general principle in zoogeography: Bergmann's rule. It is generally accepted (although there may be other reasons) that this is an adaptation because a larger animal, with a smaller ratio of surface area to volume, will lose heat less rapidly than a smaller animal. Figure 2 (page 20), based on Snow (1953, 1954), shows the relationships between the mean wing length (representing body size) of a population and the winter temperature.

The large size of the Great Tit compared with other tits, at least in colder regions, is closely related to its foraging behaviour; this species feeds on the ground more than other Palearctic tits. In this it closely parallels the Tufted Titmouse of North America, which, with a wing length of 72–85 mm (Pyle *et al.* 1987), is of comparable size and feeds on the ground more than other Nearctic tits and chickadees (Pielou 1957) illustrated on page 102. Despite the relationship between feeding sites and body size in these two species, one should not assume that large size is an adaptation to ground-foraging or vice versa, as it may have had many causes which may or may not still operate (Dhondt *et al.* 1979). Since they are less acrobatic than other tits, ground-feeding may be a related outcome rather than a driving force for natural selection. Sadly, we still know very little about the general ecology of the species in most of its range, and especially that of the smaller races.

Snow (1953) also described another general pattern of form in the Great Tit related to the size and shape of the bill. In general, larger Great Tits have larger bills, but relative to their overall size the bill lengths of birds in different populations increase with a rise in the mean temperature of the coldest month, although below about –5 °C there is no relationship, i.e., in colder climates, Great Tits have relatively shorter bills. This follows another general principle called Allen's rule: extremities – bills of birds and ears and muzzles of mammals – are smaller in colder climates, which is believed to be an adaptation to reduce heat loss. In the present case, however, this may not be the correct explanation. The Great Tit's bill shape is closely related to diet (Gosler 1987a), and this also probably varies according to winter temperature. Bergmann's and Allen's rules mean that, as is found to be the case, the largest Great Tits have the smallest bills relative to their overall size and are found in Scandinavia, while the smallest have relatively long bills and occur in south-east Asia and Indonesia. Bill depth (its vertical thickness) also increases with body size. However, the British and Irish Great Tits have a much deeper or more massive bill than expected from their body size and are recognized as a distinct subspecies *P. major newtoni*.

The most widely distributed of the allospecies is the *P. major major* group (M). This is essentially characterized by green upperparts and yellow underparts. While there is considerable variation on this basic theme (for example, birds in the eastern Mediterranean tend to be greyer), it is one of the least differentiated groups in terms of recognized geographic races. Of the eight races recognized here, the nominate *P. m. major* occurs little modified across most of the continental mass of Eurasia in a band lying between about 50 °N and 60 °N. The seven other races are more or less geographically isolated from *P. m. major*, either as island forms such as *P. m. newtoni* in Britain, *P. m. corsus* on Corsica and Sardinia and *P. m. excelsus* in North Africa, or by rugged mountains as for *P. m. aphrodite*, *P. m. terraesanctae*

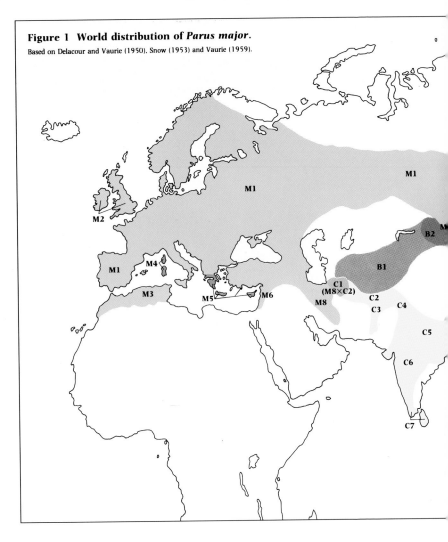

Figure 1 World distribution of *Parus major*.
Based on Delacour and Vaurie (1950). Snow (1953) and Vaurie (1959).

and *P. m. blandfordi* of south-east Europe and the Middle East. The *major* group contains some of the largest forms of the species. In Britain, for example, adult weights of 20 g are not uncommon, and fat chicks raised in ideal habitat often fledge at more than 22 g. The huge geographic range of the *major* group, with its lack of racial differentiation, reflects a rapid range extension from the west following the end of the last ice-age some 8000 years ago. The racial differentiation in the Mediterranean region suggests that this area acted as a refuge for the group during that glacial episode.

The extension eastwards of the *major* group has brought it back into contact with the descendants of Great Tit populations which were similarly cut off by the advancing ice, and isolated in central-southern and south-east Asia. The first of these, and the second allospecies, is *P. m. cinereus* (C), the range of which stretches from Afghanistan and Kashmir to India and the

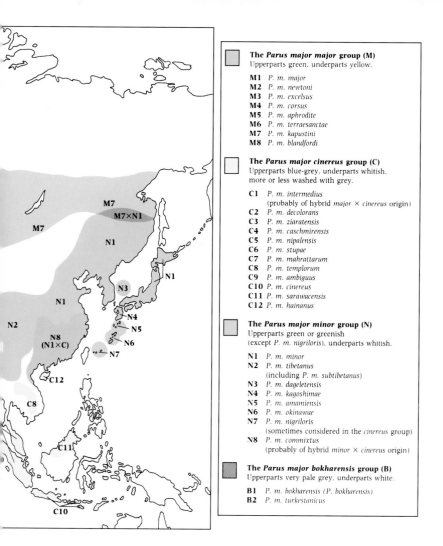

The *Parus major major* group (M)
Upperparts green, underparts yellow.

M1 *P. m. major*
M2 *P. m. newtoni*
M3 *P. m. excelsus*
M4 *P. m. corsus*
M5 *P. m. aphrodite*
M6 *P. m. terraesanctae*
M7 *P. m. kapustini*
M8 *P. m. blandfordi*

The *Parus major cinereus* group (C)
Upperparts blue-grey, underparts whitish,
more or less washed with grey.

C1 *P. m. intermedius*
    (probably of hybrid *major* × *cinereus* origin)
C2 *P. m. decolorans*
C3 *P. m. ziaratensis*
C4 *P. m. caschmirensis*
C5 *P. m. nipalensis*
C6 *P. m. stupae*
C7 *P. m. mahrattarum*
C8 *P. m. templorum*
C9 *P. m. ambiguus*
C10 *P. m. cinereus*
C11 *P. m. sarawacensis*
C12 *P. m. hainanus*

The *Parus major minor* group (N)
Upperparts green or greenish
(except *P. m. nigriloris*), underparts whitish.

N1 *P. m. minor*
N2 *P. m. tibetanus*
    (including *P. m. subtibetanus*)
N3 *P. m. dageletensis*
N4 *P. m. kagoshimae*
N5 *P. m. amamiensis*
N6 *P. m. okinawae*
N7 *P. m. nigriloris*
    (sometimes considered in the *cinereus* group)
N8 *P. m. commixtus*
    (probably of hybrid *minor* × *cinereus* origin)

The *Parus major bokharensis* group (B)
Upperparts very pale grey, underparts white.

B1 *P. m. bokharensis (P. bokharensis)*
B2 *P. m. turkestanicus*

Himalayas, east into Bangladesh and Burma, and south-east into Thailand,
Malaysia, Sumatra, Sarawak, Java and the Lesser Sundas. The *cinereus*
group is characterized by blue-grey upperparts and whitish underparts, the
whole being more or less washed with grey. Like the *major* group, it has
become differentiated into a number of races as a result of isolation on
islands, for example *P. m. ambiguus* on Sumatra and *P. m. cinereus* itself on
Java and the Lesser Sundas, or in mountain areas, an example being *P. m.
nipalensis* in the Himalayas. Where its range meets that of the *major* group
in the form of the very pale *P. m. blandfordi*, it will breed freely with it, and
this has probably resulted in the race *P. m. intermedius* which differs from
the typical *cinereus* in having a slight green nuchal/mantle spot.

    Another race believed to be of hybrid origin is *P. m. commixtus* in
China. This, however, would have resulted from interbreeding between the

A flock of Great Tits flies low over beechmast-strewn ground. So important is mast to the birds in winter, that wide-scale irruptive dispersal occurs if the crop fails.

cinereus group and the third allospecies – the *minor* group (N). The *minor* group presents a further variation on the basic theme, this time of greenish upperparts and whitish underparts. It represents a post-glacial expansion from a refuge in south-east Asia, isolated to the west by the Himalayas and to the north by inhospitable glacial and periglacial conditions. Considerable sub-specific differentiation has occurred within the isolated island populations of Japan and the Ryukyu islands, where six distinct races occur. As in *major*, however, most of the continental range of the *cinereus* group is represented by just two or three (with *P. m. commixtus*) extensive races, suggesting a rapid, post-glacial, extension of the range. Where the race *P. m. minor* meets the birds of the *major* group in the form of *P. m. kapustini* in the region of the Amur valley, the two races interbreed: a true meeting of east and west.

The fourth group is the *bokharensis* group of Turkestan (B). This is distinguished by its small size, relatively longer tail and very pale grey upperparts and white underparts. *P. m. bokharensis* has long presented a paradox to the taxonomist because, while it shares recent ancestors with *P. major*, it represents an earlier isolation than those discussed above. Hence, where they overlap in the western Himalayas, *bokharensis* and *cinereus* do not interbreed. As reproductive isolation is the main criterion used to define a species, this has led many, e.g., Sibley and Monroe (1990), to classify it as a species *P. bokharensis* (Turkestan Tit). This would be fine were it not that, in the north-east of its range, its subspecies, *P. m. turkestanicus* hybridizes with *P. m. kapustini*. This illustrates the shortcomings of our system of classification. It is ironic that, although we understand the biological basis and historical reasons for the problem, our system of nomenclature is not sufficiently flexible to accommodate it and so it remains a matter of personal preference whether to lump it with *P. major* or separate it as *Parus bokharensis*.

Other variations

Racial differences do not account for all the variation in colour in the Great Tit, because individuals within a population also differ markedly. Here I shall describe the plumage variation only of the nominate race *P. m. major*, illustrated on page 15, although such a description holds for most of the *major* group. In general, as with many other tits, males present the boldest

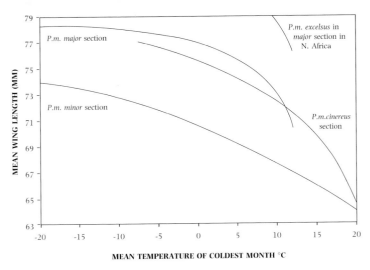

Figure 2 *Great Tit body size increases geographically with decreasing temperature. The graph shows the relationship between the average body size in a population, represented by mean wing length, and mean temperature of the coldest month for different populations in three of the Great Tit groups: major, cinereus and minor.*

and brightest plumage; females show the same general pattern but are less contrasting. In particular, the gloss of the cap and bib is reduced in the female. The belly-stripe, which in males can be extensive, jet-black, and joins the base of the legs, in females is usually much reduced, often contains white feathering (giving a greyer appearance) and frequently is replaced by white on the belly and between the legs. Apart from the admixture of white in the belly-stripe, the yellow of the underparts is often less intense in females than in males. While these differences are clearly sex-linked, they cannot be of entirely genetic origin, since diet can influence the colour.

In addition to the sexual differences, the plumage also varies with age. Juvenile plumage (grown in the nest) differs markedly from the adult (page 15). Essentially, areas which are white in the adult are yellow or yellowish in the fledgling. The black of the cap, chin and belly-stripe lacks the gloss of the adult and presents a greyer, or even greenish, tint. The belly-stripe is thin and never extends to the belly or between the legs. The lesser and median secondary wing-coverts and the primary coverts, which are slaty blue in the adult, are green or washed with green in the juvenile, and the white tips of the adult greater coverts are creamy yellow in the juvenile. The greenish juvenile primary coverts are also more pointed than the adult. In late summer, the young birds undergo an extensive body moult so by October they appear more or less like the adults. As with most passerines, however, they retain the juvenile flight feathers (remiges), the greenish primary coverts, and often the juvenile alula; many also retain one or more of the outer greater coverts. The resulting contrast between the greenish primary coverts and the slaty blue of the lesser and medians allows one to age the birds. After the first complete moult, which occurs in the following summer after the birds have bred for the first time, the plumage does not change systematically with

21

age. Nevertheless, most workers agree that Great Tits continue to become brighter with age (Perrins 1979), although this has never been measured.

From this it should be clear that individual differences between the birds result from many causes. Differences due to race, age, sex and nutrition both in and out of the nest all play a part, as does the complex interplay between these factors. For example, a bird's nutritional state can depend as much upon its social status (which can determine its access to food) as on the abundance of food itself. The recognition that 'all animals are equal, but some animals are more equal than others' has greatly enhanced our understanding of their biology in recent years, and the interaction between the birds' social ecology, nutrition and other aspects of behaviour and ecology will be recurrent themes throughout the book. Further aspects of plumage variation, its significance, and moult will be considered in later chapters.

We have seen that the worldwide distribution of the Great Tit reflects a response to catastrophic environmental changes in recent geological time, but it also reflects the present distribution of suitable habitats and the diversity of habitats that the species will tolerate. Hence, the ubiquitous nature of this species reflects its acceptance of almost any shrubby habitat that can provide a hole in which to nest. While tree holes are usually preferred, holes in walls and other man-made structures, or even in the ground, can be used. Its distribution also reflects a wide diet including a range of larval and adult invertebrates, fruits and seeds. Perhaps the only limitation is the need for a high-protein diet for the chicks. This is usually provided in the form of caterpillars, particularly of defoliating moths, but recent work in Spain shows that they can raise a healthy brood largely on the adult moths (Barba *et al.* 1988, 1989; Barba and Gil-Delgado 1990). The ecological tolerance of the Great Tit is also reflected in the fact that in most of its range it is resident. Birds from the north of Fennoscandia generally migrate south and west across the Baltic into the Low Countries each autumn (Haftorn 1950; Czaja-Topiñska 1969; Källander 1983), and there is a regular movement westwards from Russia (Schierer 1965; Berndt and Henß 1967). Even these movements, however, are not genetically programmed as are those of true migrants such as Swallows, for at Oulu, in northern Finland, Great Tits are enticed by the provision of food to stay through the long winter (Orell and Ojanen 1979) and the scale of movements from eastern Europe depends on the availability of tree seeds such as beechmast on which the tits feed in winter (Ulfstrand 1962; Perrins 1966). Seasonal, altitudinal movements take place in parts of Europe, and probably in other parts of the range also since, for example, *P. m. caschmirensis* occurs at up to 2700 m (9000 ft) and *P. m. nipalensis* up to 3600 m (11,800 ft).

The four principal 'allospecies' of the Great Tit. The Parus major major *group occurs through most of Eurasia and is characterized by green upperparts and yellow underparts. The oriental P. m. minor group is typically greenish above and whitish below. The P. m. cinereus group occurs through southern Eurasia. It is characterized by blue-grey upperparts and whitish underparts. The small birds of the P. m. bokharensis group found in Turkestan have pale grey upperparts and white underparts. This race is sometimes treated as a full species P. bokharensis.*

Parus major major

P. m. minor

P. m. cinereus

P. m. bokharensis
(Parus bokharensis)

Norman Arlott

2

THE GREAT TIT'S YEAR

FEW species experience such a variety of environmental conditions across their breeding range as does the Great Tit. Its distribution takes it from the oceanic woodlands of Ireland to the continental forests and steppelands of Siberia, from the maquis scrub of the Mediterranean to the tropical mangrove swamps of Malaysia. Since most populations are resident, many of these birds will experience profound changes in climate and length of day, and therefore in food quality and quantity, with the changing seasons. These are reflected in seasonal changes in the ecology, behaviour and social organization of the birds at any place, since these are inextricably linked with environmental conditions. In describing the Great Tit's year, therefore, it is necessary to define which Great Tits and where. Since the greater part of our knowledge of this bird comes from north-west Europe, there must inevitably be a bias towards that area, and particularly favouring the Netherlands, Britain, Belgium, Finland and Sweden (*see* preface). Important studies on social organization have been made on the race *Parus major minor* in Japan, and I shall refer to these also. It is encouraging that much of the Japanese information seems applicable to Western Europe, so a general picture painted from European observation is probably representative of the species elsewhere. While we still know very little about the Great Tit in the tropics, even on Penang Island (Malaysia), which experiences no winter and little seasonality in its heavy rainfall, the species still shows a seasonal pattern in its breeding, although egg-laying can occur from mid-March right through to mid-July (Cairns 1956). We know nothing of its social organization there.

We start this review at the moment when the clutch of six to twelve eggs hatches, and we shall follow the young birds through their first eighteen months or so. During this time, they must grow and develop, learn enough about the world to survive, undergo two moults which will place heavy demands on them for protein, survive a winter which is likely to be yet more demanding, establish a territory and/or acquire a mate, and raise one or possibly two broods of their own.

The nesting period

The hatchlings are tiny, naked and pink and weigh less than 1.5 g. During the 18–21 days that they are in the nest, they increase in weight some eightfold to tenfold, to fledge at 16–22 g with plumage fully developed. A great deal of energy and protein is required by a pair of Great Tits with a combined weight of about 36 g to raise a brood of chicks to fledging at their combined weight of perhaps 200 g. For growing chicks, lepidopteran caterpillars are the most digestible source of most of the nutrients that they require, and therefore these usually form 60–95 per cent of their diet, depending on availability. During the nestling stage, the parents may deliver more than 10,000 caterpillars to the brood. Caterpillars, however, are not equally available throughout the year, nor are they equally available in all habitats or on all tree species. In oak woods, for example, caterpillar abundance and size increase rapidly in a short pulse after the buds of the leaves on which they feed burst in the spring. For a while, caterpillars may be superabundant, but the glut does not last for long. This is because the caterpillars are committed to a race against time with the trees.

Since the tree depends on its leaves for photosynthesis, it must combat the depredations of the insects in some way. This is achieved to some extent by reducing the time over which its developing leaves are palatable to defoliating caterpillars. It does this by reducing their water and protein content and increasing the concentration in them of toxic secondary compounds, such as tannins, shortly after the leaf is formed (Feeny 1970). This means that the caterpillars must time their own hatching to coincide as closely as possible with the leaf-bud burst, and to grow to pupation as quickly as possible, and the tits must try to time their breeding to coincide with this pulse of caterpillar biomass. In Chapter 7 we shall find that, while they are remarkably good at this, neither the tits nor the caterpillars always manage to predict events successfully. A similar race against time occurs between broadleaved trees other than oaks and their defoliators, but to a lesser extent in coniferous species (Speight and Wainhouse 1989). This means that there is less of a peak in caterpillar abundance in coniferous forest: caterpillars occur there at a lower density but for a longer period of time. Because of this, caterpillars usually form a smaller proportion of the diet in conifer forest and the habitat usually supports a lower breeding density of tits than does broadleaved woodland. Breeding success is often poorer there also, but the birds can more often compensate for this by producing a second, and sometimes even a third brood (Van Balen 1973).

The date on which a particular brood hatches depends on a number of local factors (*see* Chapter 7). However, the most influential of these is the date on which the first egg of the clutch was laid, and since timing of budburst and caterpillar hatching is influenced by spring temperatures it is not surprising that more-northerly broods tend to be started later than those further south and west. Indeed, Orell and Ojanen (1983a) found that a good approximation of the mean first-egg dates for populations in Europe, in which a date of 1 represents 1 April could be obtained from the equation: mean first-egg date = $(1.58 \times$ degrees lat.$) + (0.14 \times$ degrees long.$) - 57.03$. In addition to the variation in laying and thus in hatching and fledging dates, females differ greatly in the number of eggs that they lay in a season. There are many reasons for this, which we shall examine later, but clutch size, unlike timing of laying, does not vary geographically in any systematic way (Orell and Ojanen 1983b), although it was previously thought that it did (Lack 1954).

Managed Oak woodland in lowland Britain – ideal habitat for the Great Tit. Standard trees such as Oak provide an abundance of caterpillars in May and June while the coppiced shrub layer provides insect food earlier in the spring.

Fledging

Fledging marks the start of the most hazardous period of the young birds' life. All that they have known of the world during their short lives so far has been the dark security of a tree hole or nestbox. Their sleep was punctuated only by their frantic demands for food from a visiting parent. During the last few days they had looked out at the small piece of the world that was visible from their snug residence. During the next ten to fourteen days they must gradually grow towards full independence. They must learn what to eat and where to find it, and become proficient in its manipulation. They must perfect their flying skills, and they must learn what to avoid. This is easily said. For the 20–30 per cent of young tits which fall prey to Sparrowhawks, the end is quick and unexpected. Most of these victims probably never see their assassin or hear an alarm call warning of danger, for the adult hawk, feeding his brood high in a tree-top, is as efficient a killer as the fledgling is inept. The most critical period for the juveniles lies around the time of reaching full independence. It would

Conifer forest plantation in Switzerland. The low density of caterpillars in conifer forest results in a lower breeding density of Great Tits, but the more even distribution of food (compared with Oak woodland) through the summer means that the tits more often produce a second brood here.

be wrong to think that from this point they cease to acquire experience and to learn from their neighbours, but there is now no source of food other than what they can secure for themselves. It must be during the first month of life also that the young birds become aware of the Great Tit songs in their immediate vicinity. We know this because, although Great Tit males do not learn their songs specifically from their fathers, they do learn some general song types at this time, and females seem aware of the nature of their father's song (McGregor and Krebs 1982a).

Independence

Independence is not a sudden event, although the parents decide when it should occur (Davies 1978). It is more the culmination of a process which begins in the nest, because, during the period when they are dependent on their parents, the fledglings gradually expand the proportion of food that they find for themselves. During this dependent period, the parents lead the brood to favourable feeding areas. These family parties are very noisy, and in June and July the woods ring with the incessant begging calls of young tits. From these calls they are easily found, and we can assume that predators also home in on them, since Sparrowhawks show some preference for taking tits from family parties. Surprisingly, however, the hawks usually show little preference for taking the fledglings, rather than their parents, from these parties (Geer 1982).

Full independence of the first-brood young occurs from mid-May through to the end of June depending on the year and the date that the clutch was laid, although occasionally families stay together right through

---

In Europe the Sparrowhawk is one of the most efficient predators of Great Tits. This is especially so in summer when the hawks are raising their broods largely on a diet of young tits.

to the autumn (Perrins 1979). At the end of May, the first adult males begin their annual moult, so that it is not uncommon to find males replacing primaries while they still have young to feed in the nest. Females generally begin their moult a week or so later. This moult takes some three to four months to complete, though this differs among populations, and the females tend to complete it slightly more quickly (Chapter 10). In Britain, in broadleaved woodland, few (less than 5 per cent in most years) of pairs attempt a second brood, although more do in coniferous woodland. In Continental Europe second broods are very much more common. There is then a race to raise this second brood as quickly as possible because of the changes in the food supply discussed above, so that second clutches are sometimes started even before the first brood is independent. True second clutches (rather than replacements for a lost clutch) are often laid in the same nest as the first; in one case, a female started to lay her second clutch in this way three days before the first brood had fledged (Winkel 1980). Adults that attempt a second brood generally start their annual moult about three weeks later than those which attempt only one brood (Dhondt 1973). Hence, for most of the late summer the adults are in moult. This places some stress on them, and it is also possible that their flight may be slightly impaired. As a result, they tend to remain rather inconspicuous at this time, and although they stay on or near the territory, and often expand their range a little, they show little territorial activity (Saitou 1978).

Early life

I said that there was a race for the adults to raise a second brood because of the declining quality of the food supply, but they are involved in another race also. Most studies have found that early-fledged young are far more likely to survive through to breeding locally than are later young. This is true even if one takes account of the difference in food availability to the nestlings and the consequent fact that early chicks tend to fledge at a heavier weight. This is important, because there is no point in the parents enduring the stresses of a second breeding attempt in the season if the young have no chance in their turn of being recruited to the breeding population. There is now much evidence to suggest that this difference in the likelihood of survival between early and late young is due to competition between the fledglings themselves. Earlier-fledged young have a competitive advantage because they are better developed and more experienced than the later young by the time all of them are independent. It is probably for this reason also that Sparrowhawks show some preference for later-fledged juvenile Great Tits (Geer 1982).

For the juveniles, most of the summer is spent in roving bands with other juveniles of their own and other species. Apart from various other *Parus* species, these flocks often include Long-tailed Tits, Treecreepers and Chiffchaffs. Individuals join these flocks immediately after the family flocks break up. It is not always clear, however, what the relationship is between the summer flock and the family flock, because the individuals which make up the flocks vary greatly over time. This instability in flock membership probably results partly from the many aggressive interactions which occur between their members (Hinde 1952). As implied above, the fledging date of the combatants is probably an important component in determining the outcome of these interactions (Kluyver 1971; Garnett 1976; Sandell and Smith 1991). Little is known about the movements of these juvenile flocks except that there is a net immigration into better feeding areas (Drent 1984). These movements are sometimes described as random dispersal movements because they show no preferred compass direction, but this is misleading as they are not random with respect to local features and habitats. Whilst most of these 'summer flocks' remain within a fairly small area, perhaps only 15 or 20 ha, some fledglings wander much further. For example, I have observed young birds more than 1 km from their nest sites within three weeks of fledging. Saitou (1979a) states that, within a month of its joining the summer flock, a juvenile's home range is fairly well established until autumn; and, furthermore, that the summer and autumn ranges probably develop as a subset of the family flock's range. While this may be true in some cases, it cannot always be so, because family parties tend not to cover so great an area as summer flocks, especially if the parents raise a second brood. A problem with analyses of this sort is that they are easily biased, since they miss those birds which leave the study area in which the search was made and consequently they often under- estimate the distance that the birds cover.

During this hectic period of dispersal and establishment, the juveniles also moult. This does not take so long as the adults' as it is not so extensive. As with most passerines, it involves only the body and inner wing-coverts and sometimes also the tail feathers. Although less extensive than the full adult moult, it occurs at a testing time since it usually starts only ten weeks after fledging (earlier in later-fledged young). Hence, the extent of this moult varies between individuals, and especially later-fledged juveniles show less extensive moult than earlier-fledged young (see Chapter 10).

The adjustments in composition of the juvenile summer flocks which result from interactions among their members, coupled with a growing attachment by some birds to certain parts of their range, leads, by autumn, to a certain degree of stability in the flock's composition. In autumn, by when about half of the juveniles of the year have already emigrated or perished (possibly both), two changes occur in the social organization of the population. First, many (and possibly all: Drent 1983) of the first-year males attempt to establish territories in September. This naturally results in a resurgence of territorial activity by the remaining territory-holding adult males, who need to defend their ground. It is important to realize that established males remain on their territory throughout the year if local conditions and food supplies allow it. Hence, this is an aspect of behaviour which differs considerably in populations across Europe. For example, in Israel, most adults remain territorial throughout the winter (Yavin 1987). In Britain, they do so when the winter weather is mild, so song

---

Mature Beech woods in winter. Beechmast – the seed crop of Beech – is an important food for Great Tits across Europe once insects are no longer available.

(which signals territorial ownership) can be heard at any time during winter if the weather improves. In Sweden, many of the birds migrate (Björklund *et al.* 1989). Those adults which are forced to leave their territories in winter to feed join locally foraging flocks. The formation of these flocks represents the second important change in the population's organization.

Winter flocking

Saitou (1979a) suggests that in Japan the winter flocks form from the simple addition of a territorial pair to a summer flock when the latter is within the pair's range. Hence, while this flock, which he terms a 'basic flock', has a nucleus of an adult pair, with a variable number of juveniles, there is no kin or genetic relationship among the birds involved. In this respect Great Tits differ from most other tit species (Matthysen 1990). The basic flock has two recognizable areas of activity. The first is a 'basic flock range' of up to about 4 ha which includes some favoured foraging sites. There is then a 'secondary range' where the flock overlaps with the ranges of other basic flocks to form a 'compound flock', so that the whole area over which a basic flock ranges would be from 0.7 to 15.9 ha (Saitou 1979b). While it is not clear how well this describes the situation in Europe, generally observations in Wytham would not contradict it (Hinde 1952; Morse 1978). Here, however, another situation also occurs, which we should term an 'aggregation': this is where birds congregate at an especially abundant food source, irrespective of its position relative to their territories or flock ranges. This occurs particularly when there is a good crop of beechmast, since Beech is often localized (as at Wytham). In such winters, adults may travel 500 m from their territory to feed with others

The sight of flocks of Great Tits busily searching the leaf litter for beechmast is a familiar one in late autumn when the seed crop is good.

and with large numbers of first-winter birds which would otherwise be in basic flocks. In this way, aggregations of more than one hundred birds can sometimes be seen busily turning leaves in search of mast.

Within any of these group situations (flocks or aggregations), clear linear dominance hierarchies arise. The details of these are strongly influenced by location in relation to an individual's territory or home range. This phenomenon, called 'site-related dominance', will be considered further in Chapters 5 and 6. In general, however, males are dominant over females, and adults over first-winter birds within sexes, although the situation is not always this clear-cut. The impression which I have tried to create through this account is that the relationship between territoriality and flock formation is highly fluid and depends on a number of interacting features of the population, including its density and age structure, as well as local climatic conditions and the distribution and abundance of food.

Most territories are established by January and, although they may be defended weakly in cold weather, are rapidly re-established when it gets milder. Hence, there is a resurgence of territorial activity in the spring when the winter flocks break up. This marks a dynamic period in the bird's year, but the general pattern is of the surviving first-year males fitting in around the retained boundaries of surviving adult males, who usually do not give up territory. Whatever the details, territorial boundaries are usually defined by the end of March, and indeed, in one recent, exceptionally early season in Wytham, the first egg had been laid by this time. While the function of male song in announcing territorial claims is indisputable, its role in pair formation remains controversial (Chapter 6). This is partly because it is not always clear when pairs form. Hinde (1952) and Saitou (1979c) agree that, while some pairs form within the winter flocks and some adults are already paired when they join those flocks, most pairs form after the basic flocks break up. In Britain, however, Hinde considers that most are paired by the end of February and that pairs are usually formed before the breeding territory is established. Saitou considers that pairs are usually formed between birds within the same basic flock; and Björklund et al. (1989) state that in Sweden, because of the species' migratory status there, pairs usually form after territory establishment. Clearly this is a fluid situation, and it is perhaps wrong to think of a predictable sequence of events at particular times culminating in the establishment of a pair on a defined territory.

Once the pair is established, the sequence of events is less fluid than those which preceded it. The pair chooses a nest site and the female constructs the nest. She lays one egg each day until the clutch is complete, and starts to incubate on or around the day that the last egg is laid. Incubation lasts about thirteen days, and its completion marks the end of the cycle that we have traced. Although I have referred little to the food supply in this account, it is important to recognize that the history described here is set against a backdrop of almost constantly changing resources. In some years, this results in a near-complete switch from invertebrate food in summer to seeds in winter, and this has important consequences for many aspects of the bird's biology. In the next chapter, we consider food and foraging behaviour in more detail.

3

FOOD AND FORAGING

THE ecological tolerance of the Great Tit, reflected in its great geographical range, owes much to the diversity of its diet and to the means by which this is secured. Before looking at food and foraging in more detail, it is worth considering the bird's nutritional requirements. Unfortunately, we know rather little about the Great Tit's daily requirement for specific nutrients such as vitamins and protein although we can make some informed guesses about how they might change with the seasons. For example, the calcium content of eggshell must place an unusually high demand on the female to find this element during the laying period. Similarly, since feather proteins (keratins) are rich in sulphur, it is likely that sources of sulphur-containing amino acids (such as spiders) would be sought particularly during moult and when the chicks are developing their plumage. Despite these specific nutrients, most of the bird's requirements can be summarized with respect to protein and energy (mostly provided by fat and carbohydrate), since it is the availability of these that is most likely to constrain the individual's activities. Most animal tissues are constantly undergoing a complex pattern of break-down (katabolism) and renewal (anabolism). Many of the cells which make up any individual today will have been replaced within a month, and for a small bird we can assume that few will be the same after six months. This imposes a constant demand for protein, which is the main structural component of many of these tissues.

While we know little about the Great Tit's daily protein requirement, omnivorous passerines generally cannot remain in good health for long without animal protein, although many insectivores can survive well without any vegetable matter (Berthold 1976). Calculations for other species suggest that a passerine of Great Tit size requires about 8 per cent protein by weight in its diet daily (Martin 1968). Sasvari (1988) studied the effect on Great, Blue and Marsh Tits held in captivity of a diet restricted to nuts, sunflower seeds, boiled egg, cheese, cooked meat or bacon. At the first sign that a bird was suffering from the treatment, the experiment was stopped, the bird was put on to a full diet with vitamin supplement, and the number of days since the start of the experiment was recorded. Most Great Tits showed some ill effects within one to three weeks, but it is interesting that they persisted longest on a diet of nuts and fared most poorly on bacon. These results suggested that the sources of animal protein offered were deficient in some way and that the birds required a more varied diet. However, it has often been noted that Great Tits prefer invertebrate foods when offered together with seeds (Gibb 1957; Gosler 1987b), although at very low temperatures the need for energy overrides this and the birds switch their preference to seeds (Van Balen 1980; Vestjens 1983). Although it has not been measured directly, their demand for protein undoubtedly peaks during the breeding season owing to the chicks' protein requirement for growth and development. This is suggested also by a net loss of muscle protein in breeding females during the nestling stage (Gosler 1991). Moult also is likely to require an increased protein intake.

The Great Tit's energy requirements are rather better known than are those for protein. Gibb (1957) kept a number of Great Tits in outdoor aviaries and closely monitored their daily food intake and faecal production. From the energy content of both, he calculated that they required about 1.0 kcal (about 4.2 kJ) per gram of body weight daily. This convenient figure was similar to values obtained for other passerines of similar size. This handy rough estimate, however, has been criticized for several reasons that I shall not go into. My own observations in Wytham suggest that, in midwinter, a male Great Tit weighing 19.7 g at dusk would have a lean weight of 18.1 g and would lose about 0.9 g of fat during a sixteen-hour night. Since we can make assumptions about the energy value of fat, this represents 0.5 kcal used per hour (0.03 kcal/g/hr). As the bird would have been asleep for most of that time, the resulting figure of 8 kcal used overnight is probably close to the basal metabolic rate. If its energy requirements for the remainder of the day, during which it is active, are assumed to be about 2.5 times this figure (Mertens 1977), the overall daily energy needs of our 18.1-g male will be about 8 kcal during a sixteen-hour night and 10 kcal during an active eight-hour day. This gives 18 kcal in all, which agrees remarkably well with Gibb's earlier figure, and suggests that some of the objections to it that have been raised might be unfounded.

The Great Tit's preference for invertebrate food suggests that it is principally insectivorous. This is supported by the fact that more than 135 invertebrate families have been recorded in its diet, including 32 families of moths and butterflies (especially larvae), 21 of beetles, eighteen of bugs, fifteen of flies, fourteen of wasps and allies and fourteen families of spiders (Gosler 1993). Its adaptability, however, lies in its acceptance also of a wide range of plant seeds, so that more than forty plant families are also

---

Beechmast drops to the ground in the autumn, where it forms an important winter food for many birds and small mammals. Seeds taken by Great Tits show a characteristic neat hole in the side through which the contents have been removed.

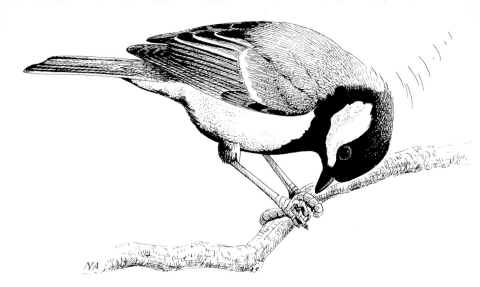

Great Tits use the same method to hold and kill caterpillars as they do to open beechmast. The item is clamped by one or both feet to a perch and hammered repeatedly with the bill.

represented. Chief among these are the seeds of hardwood trees such as Beech and, to a lesser extent, Hazel and Oak. These form the main reserve foods for the birds when the temperature drops in winter, and invertebrates become less readily available (Van Balen 1980). Indeed, so important is the crop of beechmast to some Great Tit populations that, when it fails, large-scale movements can result (Perrins 1966), but, when it is good, adult survival rates during the winter can be enhanced (Källander 1981). A relationship between juvenile survival and the quality of the beechmast crop has long been recognized in the Wytham population (Perrins 1966), but equally long has been the recognition that the relationship is, as we shall see, not a simple one (Lack 1966).

In other populations, other tree species may be more important to the tits. In south-west Ireland, for example, Terry Carruthers and I have recently noted the apparent dependence of Great Tits in winter on the seeds of Yew which, although small, have the remarkably high endosperm (the edible contents of the seed) calorific value of 8.4 kcal/g (Smal and Fairley 1980). Few other bird species in the region can make use of these seeds, because the tree protects its investment with a seed coat which is both toxic and very hard and this must be penetrated before the rich contents can be consumed. The calorific value of Yew endosperm compares favourably with beechmast, the value of which declines through the winter from 6.3 to 5.5 kcal/g (Van Balen 1980) and which may take a minute to open, and with Hazel nuts, which, although much larger and worth 7.8 kcal/g (Smal and Fairley 1980), can take ten minutes to open and five minutes to consume (Gibb 1954a). Great Tits can open Yew seeds in less than ten seconds. The time taken to open and consume these seeds is of more than just academic interest. First, time spent processing food is time that might be spent feeding on items that require less handling, so the nutritional reward for time so spent must be considered. This is particularly important in midwinter, when the birds must spend 75 per cent of their time foraging and more at the start and end of the day (Gibb 1954a). Secondly, while a tit is busy feeding on a single item it is less able to watch for predators, and, when feeding in flocks, more likely to be supplanted by a more dominant individual. For this reason, seeds, which are generally sought on the ground, are rarely processed there, but are removed to cover.

The method used to open seeds is the same as that used to kill invertebrates as diverse as caterpillars and bees. The seed or prey is clamped to a twig by one (mostly invertebrates) or both (mostly seeds) feet and is then struck repeatedly and powerfully with the strong bill. In the case of seeds, this results in a neat hole, through which the contents can be eaten. Larger seeds are sometimes wedged in a crack in a branch to gain greater purchase. Although it might not be immediately obvious, the bill itself shows several adaptations for this heavy-duty work. In particular, the thickness of keratin, the angle that the bones of the bill form with those of the skull, and the bill's depth relative to its length (bill index) all give it strength and reduce the shock to the skull. Given the strength derived from the bill's depth, it is perhaps not surprising that larger-billed Great Tits open beech seeds faster than thinner-billed ones (Gosler 1987a). The bill also changes shape through the year: it is finer in summer, when the birds switch more to an insect diet, and heavier in winter, when they turn more to seeds, and there is growing evidence that these changes are of functional value to the bird (Gosler 1987a, 1990).

Foraging behaviour

Great Tits use a number of methods to obtain food, but the well-developed co-ordination of feet and bill, together with a strong learning ability, allow great flexibility in their behaviour. Many authors have remarked on the species' intelligence compared with other small passerines, including other tits (Sasvari 1979). For example, in a series of now classic studies, Thorpe (1943) describes how captive Great Tits used the bill and feet in concert to raise a string on the end of which was tied a food item. Sasvari (1979) suggested that its intelligence probably allows the Great Tit to exploit a greater range of ecological situations and resources than other species. Three examples from the natural foraging behaviour of wild Great Tits illustrate this rather nicely. The first was recorded by Ennion (1962), who noticed that Great Tits, before expending time and energy in opening acorns, frequently tapped them with the bill and did not open all that they inspected; those that were opened usually contained a larva. Hence, the birds used this simple trick to judge whether the acorns contained live animal food. The second example has been described several times, but probably first by Gibb (1954a), and concerns the Great Tit's exploitation of the behaviour of other birds. Unlike many other *Parus* species, Great Tits do not hoard food, but they do watch the food-storing behaviour of Marsh and Coal Tits, and steal their caches after the storing bird has left. I recently watched a Coal Tit hoarding sunflower seeds in our garden: during an hour it visited about twenty sites, but few of these retained their treasure for long because of the close attention of a Great Tit. The third example is perhaps of the greatest significance, because behavioural scientists have, in the past, placed great emphasis on the use of tools as a sign of intelligence in animals. Although Great Tits frequently use the bill to extract larvae from cracks in tree bark, Duyck and Duyck (1984) watched a Great Tit using a conifer needle held in the bill to extract larvae from their holes; the needle was then discarded.

The winter dependence on tree seeds develops gradually through the autumn, so that by December plant material may make up 90 per cent of the ingested food by volume. In October, by contrast, it comprises less than 10 per cent (Van Balen 1980). Like so much of the story told here, these figures refer to northern populations, and we know rather less about winter food or foraging in warmer regions except that data from Spain suggest a much smaller reliance on plant foods there in winter (Ceballos 1972). Because of the distribution of food through the woodland profile in winter, Great Tits spend an increasing amount of their time foraging on the ground as the season progresses. For example, in November 1947 only 3 per cent of observations of feeding Great Tits in Wytham referred to the ground, while in January 1948 45 per cent did (Hartley 1953). The height distribution of the tits, however, reflects not only the distribution of food, but also constraints on their access to that food resulting from social inter-actions. From 1982 to 1985, I made a similar series of observations in Wytham to that made by Peter Hartley thirty years earlier, but I also recorded the sex of the birds concerned. Like him, I found that the tits fed on the ground more as winter progressed, but I also found that, at any given time, a majority of those on the ground were males while most females continued to search for invertebrates in the bare trees (Gosler 1987a). This sex difference in foraging, with males on the ground busily turning leaves in search of beechmast, and females probing crevices in the bark for pupae etc., resulted from the females being excluded from mast by the socially dominant males. The difference was even mirrored in the shape and size of their bills, since the males had heavier but shorter bills than the females. In Chapter 1, I drew a comparison between the feeding height and body size of the Great Tit and that of the Tufted Titmouse of North America. It is interesting that one third of the latter's diet also consists of plant matter and that most of that material is mast taken from the ground between November and February, but the social organization of the Tufted Titmouse is very different from that of the Great Tit (Pielou 1957; Matthysen 1990).

As winter draws to a close, the tits spend less time searching on the ground. In some years, this drops from 90 per cent in February to 2 per cent by June (Gibb 1954a). This is partly because there are new insect foods becoming available in the canopy of the shrub layer (especially in Hawthorn, the buds of which break early), but also because the seed supply has become so depleted over winter by small mammals and the birds themselves that the time taken to find seeds makes them no longer profitable. If the mast supply runs out before alternative foods are available,

When searching for camouflaged prey on the upperside of a leaf, Great Tits often inspect the underside for the prey's silhouette cast by the sun against the leaf. Once an insect has been found, the tit swiftly reaches over and takes it.

the birds leave the woods (Gibb 1954b). In such situations, the subordinate first-year females are the first to leave, while the dominant adult males leave last (Gosler 1987a). In years with a poor mast crop, and in coniferous woodland, the density of birds tends to be lower, so competition for resources in winter may be less intense and the tits maintain smaller feeding flocks, often with a greater range of other species. In relation to this, several workers have noted a greater tendency for Great Tits to forage in flocks when food is scarce (Morse 1978; Grubb 1987; Székely *et al.* 1989). The benefits of flocking are considered in Chapter 5. Despite these changes in behaviour, artificial food supplies such as those provided by birdtables may be very important to the tits when natural food is scarce. When natural food is available, they switch to their main foraging method of searching for invertebrates in the trees on and among leaves, in leaf rolls, on twigs and branches, behind bark and in buds, indeed wherever potential prey might be lurking. In this they show great agility, often perching on the smallest of twigs, now hanging upside-down with legs extended as if unable quite to take the weight, now hovering in short bursts, all to inspect every possible surface. Most prey will be small insects and spiders which require a minimum of processing, but as caterpillars become available in spring, and especially when foraging for the chicks, prey are increasingly 'clamped' and despatched in the manner described above, or held in the bill and repeatedly struck on a twig.

As spring gives way to summer, leaf-surface gleaning gains in importance, from about 4 per cent in April to more than 80 per cent of all feeding observations from June to August (Gibb 1954a). Although other insects, and particularly aphids and other small bugs, may be important at this time, caterpillars form the bulk of the prey taken in spring. For many broods, these form over 80 per cent of their diet, whether in Oak woods in Germany (Bösenberg 1964) or Britain (Royama 1970), in mixed woodland in Turkey (Kiziroglu 1982) or in temperate evergreen broadleaved forest in Japan (Eguchi 1980). As the caterpillar numbers decline again, the parents are forced to forage in a wider variety of sites, and to bring a greater range of prey to the young, so that late broods often receive more beetles, flies and spiders than do earlier broods (Royama 1970; Gosler 1987c). Although the search for caterpillars leads many pairs into the canopies of high-forest trees such as Oak, for much of the year there is a heavy dependence for food on the canopy of the shrub understorey, and in many studies, more than 40 per cent of the birds' foraging occurred there. Hence, Great Tits generally feed lower than other tits in the same wood.

The range of foraging behaviour and the diversity of sites inspected by Great Tits in their search for food might give the impression that their *modus operandi* is essentially random, that there is no order to their pattern of search, but this is far from the case. At its simplest, we have already seen that they did not open every acorn that they encountered when searching for larvae. There are also other tricks which help them to find prey. Many caterpillars feed on the upper surface of leaves but avoid detection by being cryptically coloured. Great Tits frequently overcome this by inspecting the undersides of the leaves against the sky, since an object on the upper surface casts a shadow which is more easily seen through the leaf; the tit then turns to the upper surface and swiftly takes the insect. However, their pattern of search is yet more complex than this. A Great Tit's environment is structured at many levels: leaves within branches, branches within trees and shrubs, and trees within the territory, so food is distributed neither evenly nor randomly, but in patches. Since time is precious to the foraging bird if it is to obtain sufficient food, it must order its search so that it concentrates on the most productive patches and, most importantly, does not spend too long in a patch when moving to another might be more profitable. Such an ordered strategy, in which a bird optimizes its use of foraging time, is called 'optimal foraging'. A great deal of research over the last fifteen to twenty years indicates that Great Tits (and most other birds studied) follow precise rules when foraging, which allow them best to budget their time (see Stephens and Krebs 1986 for a review). While it would not be appropriate to go into depth on this here, many exciting results in this field have come from work on the Great Tit and a short review is worthwhile.

Great Tits clearly learn to recognize the most productive patches. In the laboratory, if presented with feeding 'patches' of different quality, they first sample all, and then concentrate on the most profitable (Smith and Dawkins 1971; Krebs *et al.* 1978a). When feeding a brood, parents make repeated visits to the same area, returning with 'runs' of prey of the same type, before switching patch and prey (Royama 1970; Smith and Sweatman 1974). How long should the bird spend in a given patch before switching? The solution to this problem is quite simple to determine mathematically if one knows the average patch quality for the area in question and the average distance (or travel time) between patches. As the tit forages in a patch and removes food from it, so the remaining food becomes increasingly hard to find. The rate at which it finds food therefore declines from the time that it enters and starts to forage in the patch. To determine the optimal giving-up time for the patch, the tit must balance this change in the rate of gain against the time that it will need to travel to another patch (i.e., the greater the distance between patches, the longer the bird should stay in a patch). If it gives up before the optimal point is reached, it would be wasting feeding time by travelling. If it stays longer, it would gain less extra food from the patch than if it moved on to a new one. The optimal solution may, therefore, differ between territories depending on the average quality and distribution of patches in the territories. If the average quality of patches is poor, it should spend less time in each patch than if it is good. The mathematical solution to this problem is known as the 'marginal value theorem' (Charnov 1976). In the laboratory, Cowie (1977) found that the 'giving-up times' of Great Tits foraging in artificial patches were remarkably close to those predicted by this theorem.

A similar argument can be used to determine the balance between the size of prey that parents should bring back to the nest and the distance they must go to find it. This 'central-place foraging' model (foragers return to the same location) is similar to the marginal value theorem, but here birds do not gain more by searching longer in a patch. Instead, the time in the patch reflects the tit's chance of finding a larger caterpillar (Orions 1980). For example, suppose that territories differ in the distance between patches but not in the probability that, by searching longer, the bird might find a larger caterpillar once it has entered the patch. In a territory where patches are close together, a tit should spend less time searching before moving to another patch than in a territory where patches are more widely dispersed. That wild Great Tits do this is suggested by the fact that individuals which travel farther from the nest return with larger prey (Royama 1970).

In foraging optimally, it is also necessary for the birds to reject some of the insects that they find, either immediately in favour of others, or in the 'hope' (based on experience) of finding better. To judge correctly, they must balance the nutritional gain of any given prey item against the time taken to find, identify and process that prey, given that, while larger caterpillars yield more protein and calories, they also take longer to kill and the trade-off between these varying conditions is not necessarily a direct one. The nutritional value of a prey type relative to its abundance and processing time represents its profitability. In a series of experiments to study the food preferences of captive Great Tits in relation to relative profitability, Krebs *et al.* (1977) found that, if food was scarce, the birds were unselective in their

41

Blue Tit

Azure Tit

Marsh Tit

Willow Tit

Sombre Tit

Siberian Tit

Crested Tit

Coal Tit

Great Tit

Norman Arlott

choice and took anything available; as their rates of encountering different prey types increased, however, they increasingly selected more profitable ones, ignoring less profitable prey even if these were more abundant. Erichsen *et al.* (1980) later showed that, if the better prey were harder to recognize, the tits would switch to poorer but more easily recognized food rather than wasting time trying to discriminate between prey types if the relative profitability of the poorer prey was greater because of its shorter discrimination time. Houston *et al.* (1980) showed that if they were unable to distinguish prey types, or if it took a long time to discriminate between prey because they were cryptic, the birds gave up trying to specialize.

Wild Great Tits frequently specialize on particular prey species when feeding a brood, and this supports the view that experiments on captive birds are relevant and can help us understand their natural behaviour. Indeed, several authors have noted that the proportion of the diet made up by certain cryptic prey species is greater than that in which they are naturally found, and it has been suggested that the tits might develop a mental picture or 'search image' for these prey (see Perrins 1979). The problem with this idea is that a concentration on particular prey species might be achieved by other means. For example, if such prey are more profitable, perhaps because they are more common, the bird might learn to spend more time searching each patch for them (Guildford and Dawkins 1987). The problem with this 'search-rate' hypothesis is that it does not necessarily predict that a particular prey species would make up a greater proportion of the bird's diet than that in which it was found. Alternatively, the bird might have a specific range of sites in which it searches, which makes it more likely to find those prey species which inhabit such sites. Recent studies with captive Willow Tits and Great Tits suggest that different species do indeed specialize on different types of feeding site, and this need not involve the development of a search image (Suhonen and Inki 1992).

It might seem remarkable that these birds follow such complex strategies when foraging, and one might wonder how they cope with the mathematics necessary! But of course, they do not need to calculate solutions to foraging problems, any more than they need to understand aerodynamics to be able to fly, or we need to understand gravity to be able to walk. It is built into their neural circuitry just as the machinery necessary to co-ordinate our own muscles is built into ours. Ydenberg (1984) found that in fact the tits used quite simple rules of thumb, based on the time since they last found a prey item, to determine when to give up in a patch, and it seems likely that other simple rules lie behind many of these complex decisions.

The nine tit species of the Western Palearctic. The Great Tit is the largest tit in the region. These are all agile little birds which use a diverse array of postures to reach food. However, the larger size of the Great Tit constrains its foraging somewhat so that it feeds more regularly from the forest floor than other species. This is especially so in winter when tree seeds like beechmast form its principal food.

4

THE GREAT TIT POPULATION

WHY is there the number of Great Tits that there is at any given place and at any given time? The quest to answer this apparently simple question has lain at the heart of much of the research on this species for over fifty years, like some sort of ecological Holy Grail. This is because, while there may be no particular merit in predicting the abundance of Great Tits next year in Wytham or the Hoge Veluwe, since they are unlikely to become either a pest or a case for conservation, there is merit in understanding the mechanisms and principles which determine their numbers. It is worth restating the two characteristics of the Great Tit that make it particularly suitable for such studies. These are its use of nestboxes and the fact that, at least in the western populations, it remains within its breeding range throughout the year. The advantage of nestboxes is that, if they are placed at a sufficiently high density within a study site, so great a proportion of the population will take to using them that one needs only to check a prescribed set of sites to find most of the breeding attempts in that area. This virtually eliminates the need to search for nests, which is labour-intensive and also risks revealing the nest to predators by the clearance of vegetation to allow regular inspection of its contents.

Here arises a fundamental criticism of such studies, and it is as well to come clean from the outset. The use of nestboxes makes it possible to study this species more completely and in a way that reduces disturbance by the observer, but it may introduce new forms of bias. Birds using nestboxes may run a lower risk from predators than they would in natural sites, but this depends very much on the design of the box (Dunn 1977; Perrins 1979). Wooden boxes nailed directly onto a tree probably suffer predation rates which are as high as or higher than natural sites, while suspended concrete boxes are virtually immune to predation (*see* overleaf). Birds in nestboxes may produce a more consistent clutch size than they would in natural sites (Löhrl 1973, 1980, 1986; Van Balen 1984) and they may suffer less from parasites (Møller 1989). In some woods, nestbox density might influence patterns and densities of settlement (Kluijver 1951; Minot and Perrins 1986), although this is not always so (Drent 1987). It has even been suggested that in one population the use of nestboxes has reduced the average size of the Great Tits themselves: this is because the presence of boxes reduced the competition for nest sites, and that competition had favoured larger birds (Dhondt *et al.* 1979). However, none of these factors has yet been shown to affect the overall number of birds breeding in a wood in subsequent years, because their influence is small compared with

A pair of Great Tits visit their brood in a wooden nestbox. While the use of nestboxes has revolutionized the study of these birds care must be taken when interpreting the results.

other factors which influence survival rates. While it is important that we take into account as many effects as we can, and certainly the recognition of such problems opens up whole new vistas of research, the fact is that without nestboxes there would be far less work undertaken on hole-nesting passerines. To see the importance of this, one needs only compare the scale of research on the breeding biology of the Great or Blue Tits with that on the Willow Tit or the Nuthatch which show less interest in boxes.

Population sizes

In later chapters, we shall look in some detail at the factors which are known to influence the numbers of Great Tits. This chapter introduces some general principles of ecology and evolutionary biology that will feature significantly, later in the book. Many of these principles are better

Concrete nestboxes, such as this example at Wytham, are now used in many Great Tit population studies as they are proof against most predators. A plastic hat helps to defeat even the most persistent Weasels.

understood because of Great Tit studies. First, we should define 'population' and ask whether populations are phenomena with real biological meaning or whether they are merely created in the minds of ecologists for our own convenience. A population is a group of animals or plants defined (and therefore recognized) by characteristics which we select. Usually, as in this case, these characteristics describe the species involved, the time and the location. Hence, we might refer to the Great Tit population of Wytham Woods in 1993, the human population of Britain in 1824 or the population of all waders on the Wash in January 1982. The important point is that a population is defined by those characteristics of time, space and genetic constitution which meet the needs of the researcher. This has important implications, as artificial limits (space, time or genetics) are not recognized by the birds. For example, if we refer to the population of Great Tits in a 10-ha block of woodland within a larger forest, we may find it difficult to account for changes in density if birds move freely in and out of the area and if mortality is influenced by factors such as the quality of the beechmast crop in another part of the forest. This suggests that a population's boundaries have biological relevance if they are recognized by the birds also. It is, therefore, biologically meaningful to talk about the Great Tit population of Britain, because there is little passage of birds across its defined boundaries. This isolation has resulted in the evolution of a more or less distinct subspecies in Britain. This suggests that we may recognize populations as real if they are not genetically continuous with those in surrounding areas, i.e., if there is no 'gene flow'. The problem is that Britain is too large an island for its entire Great Tit population, probably of 10–15 million birds (Gosler 1986), to be studied. So we must define smaller populations that vary in their degree of artificiality.

The most obvious boundaries in the Great Tit's environment (obvious to us, at least) are abrupt changes in habitat type: the edge of a wood, perhaps, or the change from conifer plantation to ancient semi-natural woodland. Such boundaries are not always so clear-cut since, under natural conditions, woodland grades to grassland via scrub, which may not offer nesting opportunities to the tits in the spring, but may offer food in autumn. Nevertheless, most Great Tit population studies focus on the birds of a particular woodland estate with clear limits and in which nestboxes have been provided, but it is recognized that the population is not closed to immigration or emigration. It is generally the size of the *breeding* population which is considered because this is the group for which we can make our most accurate census estimate. In non-migratory populations, it is also the most stable group of birds from year to year, since, although many breeding birds are immigrants, once they have established a territory males rarely reject it in favour of another unless nearby (Kluijver 1951; Krebs 1971), and successful pairs rarely divorce (Kluijver 1951; Perrins and McCleery 1985). In migratory populations such as those in Sweden, the situation may be more fluid (Björklund *et al.* 1989).

Because most of the Great Tits in these populations breed in nestboxes, and their chicks are ringed before fledging, immigrants can be recognized as those birds not ringed as nestlings (Clobert *et al.* 1988; McCleery and Clobert 1990). This reveals that about half of the breeding birds in any study wood in any year were not hatched there. While true of mainland sites (Van Noordwijk and Van Balen 1988; McCleery and Clobert 1990), this is clearly influenced by a site's isolation: in the Dutch island population of Vlieland, only 20 per cent of breeding birds are immigrants (Van Balen *et al.* 1987). For sites not geographically isolated, we assume that there is a more or less free movement of birds into and out of the population, so immigration tends to balance emigration. Should we expect this, since not all habitats are equally suitable? If we take Wytham Woods as an example, clearly the wood should be a much better place for tits to breed than the surrounding farms and nearby city of Oxford, and yet the overproduction of young that occurs there each year (on average, five young for each future vacancy) seems not to maintain the population without a significant immigration. This is because, while the wood is the best place to breed, it may not be the best place to feed in high summer and autumn, when most juveniles die and when much of the territorial behaviour occurs that will influence the size of the breeding population (Drent 1983; Tinbergen *et al.* 1987). Thus a great deal of mixing occurs at this period between young birds born within the population (residents or autochthonous if they stay) and those born outside (immigrants or allochthonous if they enter the population). From the presence of unringed juveniles in Wytham in late June, it seems that this mixing occurs as soon as the broods are independent. This movement also has a bearing on the genetic make-up of the population, because such a flow of birds across population boundaries means there are no limits to gene flow. The importance of immigration in maintaining population density must also be related to the size of the site. Bäumer-März and Schmidt (1985) found that many populations in small woods near Frankfurt could only be sustained by significant immigration.

Great Tit populations show long-term stability, despite variation over time in birth and death rates and in levels of immigration and emigration. For example, between 1960 and 1990 the Wytham population varied from 110–350 pairs, but in most years there are about 200–250 pairs and the numbers appear to oscillate around this level. This observation leads to the conclusion that the population is in some way self-regulating i.e., that the strength of influence that births, deaths and movements have on overall numbers is related to the density of the population itself. For example, if mortality acts density-dependently in such a way that it regulates numbers, a greater proportion of the population would die when density is high than when it is low. Only density-dependent factors can have such a regulating effect. Several parameters operate in this way in Great Tit populations.

Generally, territorial behaviour limits the number of Great Tit pairs in an area, but territory size is not itself fixed, either for the species or within a site, in such a way that it prevents the population from varying over time. For example, Drent (1983) found that if potential settlers arrived in a vacant space simultaneously more stood a chance of establishing territory than if they arrived at different times. Also, in some populations, not all breeding pairs are territorial. Eyckerman (1974) and Dhondt and Schillemans (1983) have described a situation in Belgium where birds arrive already paired in another pair's territory, occupy a nestbox and raise a brood apparently without being challenged; they then leave the wood with their brood. These 'guest' pairs seem to be tolerated by the territory-holders, although the guests usually behave inconspicuously by not singing and by flying in and out of the territory near the ground and along its boundaries where possible. In one wood of 11.7 ha, which contained 118 nestboxes, 46 pairs bred but of these only 27 were known to have defended a territory before. While the breeding success of guest pairs is often poorer than that of territory-holders, the subsequent survival of their young seems no worse. Guest pairs have not been found in Wytham (East and Perrins 1988).

Guest pairs seem most likely to occur in good habitat with a surplus of nest sites. They therefore represent an extreme case of the trend that breeding density increases with improving habitat quality. For example, while Belgian Oak woods with their high caterpillar densities can support breeding densities of 39.3 pairs per 10 ha, the more mixed woodlands of Wytham support 6.5–12.9 pairs (Minot and Perrins 1986) and coniferous woodland in the Netherlands only 1–4 pairs per 10 ha (Van Balen 1973). In general, habitats which have been more modified by man are of poorer quality and hold lower densities: e.g., 1.4–4.5 pairs per 10 ha in city gardens in Cardiff (Cowie and Hinsley 1987), 5–18 pairs in Spanish orange groves (Gil-Delgado and Barba 1987) and 4–18 pairs in a range of poorer park and woodland habitats in Belgium (Dhondt 1987). There are exceptions to this trend, and the highest density yet of 51 pairs per 10 ha was recorded in German allotments (Berressem et al. 1983) and the lowest of 0.1–2.8 pairs per 10 ha is in the last remaining primary broadleaf-forest habitats of Europe, in the Bialowieza National Park, Poland (Tomialojc et al. 1984). What mechanisms result in the birds spacing themselves out in this way? The most simple suggestion is that they occupy a territory consistent with the amount of food in it. Hence, in poorer habitats, each territory would be larger so there would be fewer of them. Although there may be some truth in this, there is little evidence for it. Kluijver (1951) found that 'domiciles' (the area in which birds bred and roosted) of Great Tits differed little in mixed and conifer woodland. While breeding densities differed in the two habitats, domiciles were usually of 3 or 4 ha and never more than 10 ha. It is inconceivable that they should defend territories of the size required to account fully for the densities in Bialowieza. Kluijver also noted, as have many others, that woods often contain unoccupied space which appears suitable. Krebs (1971) found that, while territory boundaries varied greatly between years, this was because of interactions between the birds concerned rather than because of changes in habitat quality.

Brown (1969) suggested that, when territories were available, those in the best habitat were filled first, those in poorer habitat next and the poorest ones last. This would explain Kluijver and Tinbergen's (1953) observation that breeding density varied less in high-quality habitat. Krebs (1970) found that, as the breeding population increased in Wytham, so the proportion that was in poorer habitats increased also. However, this does not entirely explain why the birds settle at the densities they do. Fretwell (1972) put forward a solution for which there is also supporting evidence (Lemel 1989a): that the birds settle according to an 'ideal free distribution' (overleaf). Fretwell's argument hinges on the observation, which has been made in many Great Tit studies, that breeding productivity declines with an increasing density of pairs (negatively density-dependent). As the density increases, there comes a point where a pair could do as well or even better by breeding in a poorer habitat but at a lower population density. If this does indeed explain the differences in density between different habitats, it raises many questions. Why does productivity decline with density in a given habitat? How do the birds balance their decision to breed in a particular habitat against the density of birds there, and how do they know what would be the best density for a given habitat in a given year anyway?

Clearly important in this debate is how space becomes available in a population, as a surviving male usually retains his territory. This means that, unless the population was at a low with free space to start with, settlement concerns filling space left by the death of a territory-holder. It has been shown in several populations that on average about half of the breeding adults die before the next breeding season. In fact, it is usually more than half of the females, and under half of the males. The causes seem unrelated to age, although birds over six years old are less likely to survive another year (McCleery and Perrins 1988). This means that, irrespective of the qualities that determine which juveniles survive until autumn, whether or not they are able to establish a territory will depend partly on the free space available for them because they will not usually oust an established territory-holder. Drent (1987) found that the density of established juvenile males in September could be approximated by the equation: $6.52 - (0.77 \times$ density of territorial adult males$) + (0.21 \times$ density of competing juvenile males$) =$ density of established juvenile males. Hence, the density of established juveniles is density-dependent; the adult density tends to reduce it, while it tends to be increased by overall juvenile density. These results are consistent with earlier observations that changes in overall population density from year to year are positively related to the proportion of first-year birds in the population in winter and that, for some reason, this is itself related to the abundance of beechmast at that time (Perrins 1965). While food supply is involved in the survival of the tits and thus in population regulation, it seems that predation is not. Between 1959 and the early 1970s, Sparrowhawks were absent from Wytham because of pesticides. Also, since the mid 1970s, the number of clutches and broods lost to Weasels has been reduced by replacing wooden nestboxes with concrete ones. Despite dramatic changes in predation levels, the population's dynamics seem virtually unaltered (McCleery and Perrins 1991).

The fact that populations show internal regulation does not mean that density-dependent factors operate in some way for this purpose. For that to be true, we should have to argue that density-dependence is an adaptation to prevent population density from being too large or too small, either of which could lead to the population going extinct owing to lack of resources or catastrophic events such as hard weather. The reason for resisting such an idea is that the situation could not have evolved by natural selection.

Genetic influences

Each individual carries a genetic blueprint in its cells. This 'genome' is unique and determines many aspects of the bird's structure and appearance, behaviour and interaction with its environment. The combined genetic variation of the population constitutes its gene pool. A common feature of many Great Tit populations is that they produce far more fledged young than could be sustained by the local environment. At Wytham, 64 per cent of breeding females recruit no young into the population (McCleery and Perrins 1988). The equivalent figure for Hoge Veluwe is 57 per cent, and Vlieland is 42 per cent (Van Balen *et al.* 1987). The lower value for Vlieland reflects reduced emigration, so there is a greater chance of a female's offspring being found breeding within the study area. In the Dutch populations, half of all recruits were produced by 11 per cent of breeding females. Clearly, many young die before their first breeding season. If the set of fledglings that survived to breed was a random sample with respect to genetically determined traits such as body size, date of fledging, size of clutch from which they came, etc., we should not see any change in such characteristics in the breeding population in subsequent years, but the survivors are not a random selection: they are often the heaviest chicks, or the earliest-fledged ones, or those from a clutch-size close to the commonest in the population. The gene pool of the subsequent breeding population is thus made up of such birds, and as a result of that 'natural selection' is slightly different from the whole 'cohort' of chicks that was produced. Evolution has taken place, albeit on a small scale.

The factors that select for particular characteristics do not necessarily select the same characteristics every year, nor do they always select them so strongly. For example, when the population density is high, competition for resources may favour larger individuals. If body size is inherited, and if

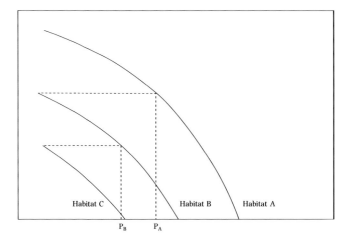

AVERAGE BREEDING SUCCESS

Habitat C   Habitat B   Habitat A

P_B P_A

POPULATION DENSITY

Figure 3 *When should a bird move to a poorer habitat to breed? One solution is the 'ideal free distribution' illustrated by this graph (based on Fretwell 1972). This assumes that average breeding success of birds in a habitat declines with increasing population density (indicated by the solid curves). Curves relating breeding success and density are shown for three habitats: 'A', 'B' and 'C' in which 'A' is better than 'B', which is better than 'C'. If the density of birds in A exceeds PA a bird might be more successful in a poorer habitat ('B') if the density there is low. If the density there exceeds PB, the bird might fledge more young if it moved into a yet poorer habitat where fewer birds are attempting to breed.*

this competition results in the deaths of smaller birds, the average body size of the survivors will have been selected to be larger. In another year, however, population density and competition may be less, the selection for body size may be relaxed, and the average size of survivors may be smaller because proportionately more small individuals were able to survive. Thus natural selection results in birds that are adapted to yesterday's conditions. If those conditions prevail, then they are better adapted today also, but, if conditions change, the fittest set of birds may be different again. Evolution by natural selection also means that characteristics of the population such as density-dependent mortality cannot evolve (and therefore are not adaptive), because they cannot arise through the selection of individuals. The genetic variation upon which selection operates arises through mutations in the genome occurring randomly. However, while the variation arises at random, the selection itself is not. Natural selection results in plants and animals which 'aim' to maximize their own chances to have their young recruited into the breeding population and so to have their own genes in the population's gene pool. When we ask why a Great Tit behaves in a particular way, we should consider how its actions improve those chances; in other words, how they improve its lifetime reproductive success or fitness.

5

JOINING THE FLOCK

ALTHOUGH Great Tits are strongly territorial during the breeding season, and males may remain so through the winter if conditions allow it, many of them form or join flocks outside the breeding season. The next chapter considers the nature and function of the territory further, but first we shall look at the winter flocks. We have already seen (Chapter 2) that these flocks often have their origins back in the summer. These developed from the bands of roving juveniles which, through a process of aggressive encounter leading to emigration and death, have by October been more or less halved in number. I stressed earlier that, during the following period, social organization is fluid and the birds' distribution by territories or flocks depends on weather conditions, food availability and status, so this may differ markedly among populations. The composition and behaviour of the winter flocks have been studied mostly in Britain and the Netherlands, with important studies also in Japan and Hungary. The European studies tell much the same story, and while there are differences in details from Japan the story there is similar. While this gives some confidence that there are similarities across the range, there is still great scope for work on social organization elsewhere, and especially in southern Europe, where the birds may be more strongly territorial in the winter (Yavin 1987), and in tropical populations, about which we know virtually nothing.

Hinde (1952) described in detail the nature and behaviour of the winter flocks. True flocks differ from aggregations (Chapter 2) in that they have a clear coherence, although it is not always possible to distinguish between the two. Hinde noted that true flocks move slowly through the wood in an integrated way, so that all the birds move together to a new feeding place. There are no clear leaders in such movements, and the flock may move 180 m in a single flight. In this way they may move up to 220 m per hour, with a mean rate of about 100 m per hour. On average, the flock would patrol an area of about 4 ha and appeared to be more integrated in the mornings and between November and January than at other times. Although many birds may be involved in aggregations also, because they have gathered at a static food source, the individuals do not behave in so organized a way. Flocks are usually smaller in size than aggregations and are more likely to contain other species. Morse (1978) found Great Tits in half of the mixed-species tit flocks that he observed in Wytham, and on average, when present, there were only two Great Tits per flock. This agrees with Saitou's (1978) findings that the basic flock of Great Tits (Chapter 2) consisted of between two and sixteen birds depending on the number of first-years included, and that this unit showed a stable membership. I have, however, watched very much larger Great Tit flocks than this in Wytham, and Hinde (1952) considered that flocks of fifty were not uncommon. It is not clear how stable the membership of Great Tit flocks is in Europe.

Why do Great Tits flock? There are two sides to this question, because, if the alternative to flocking is territoriality, we might equally ask why they defend territories? I shall return to that question in the next chapter, but it may be useful to think of flocking behaviour in this polarized way. Since natural selection produces adaptive solutions (Chapter 4), we can expect an individual's behaviour (to flock or not to flock) to reflect a balance of costs and benefits. Ultimately, these costs and benefits are measured in terms of the total number of the bird's offspring that subsequently breed themselves (the lifetime reproductive success or fitness in Chapter 4), but the survival of the individual itself is an important contributor to that success. Put simply, if the bird does not survive the winter, it can not breed next year. So, if the costs to a bird's chances of surviving of some behaviour – such as flocking – outweigh the benefits, it may leave fewer offspring in the next generation carrying the genes that cause that behaviour. Since this process must have been going on for thousands of generations, gradually moulding behaviour, we can now ask what are the benefits of flocking under the conditions in which it occurs, and what are the costs which maybe cause birds to stop flocking when territoriality prevails.

The benefits of flocking

Ornithologists have recognized two principal benefits to be gained by joining a flock. The first is in terms of predator avoidance. Many pairs of eyes are simply more likely to detect a predator than is one pair. Any individual while feeding must budget some time to looking out for predators. Watch any tit on a garden peanut feeder: it takes a few pecks, then looks up before pecking again. When it looks up in this way, it is surveying for predators. Such vigilance costs feeding time. If more birds are looking for predators, any one bird can afford to look up less often from feeding but maintain the same overall probability of detecting a predator. The flock's eyes are of course also more widely distributed than the individual's, and this, too, may improve the chance of detecting a predator. So, flocking can increase the feeding rates of birds by reducing the need for vigilance, but this system can work only if the bird can rely on its flock-mates to give a warning call if a predator is detected, and giving an alarm runs the risk to the caller that it will make itself more conspicuous to the predator. As a result, high-frequency alarm calls have evolved in many flocking species. These are reserved for response to avian predators such as Sparrowhawks. In the Great Tit, this call is around 7–8 kHz (song is usually below 5.5 kHz) and may be described as 'seeee'. Such calls minimize this risk to the caller because they are difficult to pinpoint. Lower-frequency 'pink', 'tink' and 'churrr' calls are reserved for slower-moving or less immediately threatening risks such as mammal predators. The calls differ in this way because the most appropriate responses differ in the two situations. In the latter case, the flock members usually flee to cover. The most appropriate response to the 'seeee' call is to freeze motionlessly unless in a very exposed location;

Great Tits at a peanut feeder. Such food can make a significant difference to the birds in winter, but it may provide a focus for predators also, so the birds must always be vigilant.

a tit caught out on a feeder when this call is given will often appear confused because of the conflict between whether to freeze or flee.

The second benefit to be gained from flocking is often referred to as 'social enhancement'. This suggests that flocking individuals can learn more quickly about the distribution of food in the flock's range by watching their flock–mates. That is, they can learn from the experiences of others. Krebs *et al.* (1972) and Krebs (1973) tested this idea in a series of aviary experiments with Great Tits and with two species of North American chickadees. They found that the birds were more likely to inspect a type of site for prey if they had seen others finding prey in such sites, and therefore that individuals in groups found food in the aviary more quickly than when alone. Krebs *et al.* (1972) also noted, however, that social status played a part in determining how much food an individual consumed. Baker (1978) pointed out that, although the feeding rates of all the birds in these groups were enhanced, dominant birds benefited most because they parasitized subdominant individuals. They did this by using the 'supplanting attack', in which the (usually) socially dominant bird attempts to land on another's perch at the exact place where the latter is feeding. Such attacks are usually successful in that the feeding bird is replaced by the supplanter. While this may benefit the aggressor at a feeder, however, in the flock situation it often results in the feeding bird dropping the food item that it had clamped between its feet, so that neither bird benefits. This, then, is the cost of flocking. There is a balance, that must be assessed by each bird, between the benefits which arise through predator avoidance and social enhancement and the costs (or benefits?) which can accrue from its own status. Baker suggested that there may come a point, perhaps related to the flock's size, when a subdominant bird might be better off if it left the flock.

To what extent is flocking behaviour influenced by predator avoidance or social enhancement in free-living Great Tits? Grubb (1987) attempted to answer this question by assessing the proportion of the population in flocks in Holly Wood, near Oxford. Through January and February, he alternated providing large quantities of food for about a week with removing the food for a similar period. Food was provided so that dominant individuals could not monopolize it. This procedure gave two periods with food and three without. Sparrowhawks were seen in the wood throughout the period. Great Tits were more likely to flock at low temperature, but this was not seen when food was provided. After taking the weather into account, he found that Great Tits with access to food were less likely to join mixed-species flocks when provisioned. Females were more likely to flock when food was removed and more often visited feeders than did males, because males were reluctant to leave their territories. Males, however, were better able than females to handle the Hazel nuts in the wood, so they probably had an alternative food supply. In addition, the density of Great Tits in the wood increased when food was provided because of an influx of birds, especially males, from outside. At this time, males outnumbered females in the wood, while the reverse was true when food was removed. However, the addition of food had no effect on the formation of single-species flocks. The effects of adding food on the propensity of the birds to flock implicate social enhancement as a major factor, but, as I noted above, reduced vigilance also results in more time for feeding, so it is not a simple matter to distinguish between these effects. Sasvari (1992) pointed out that subdominant Great Tits could benefit more from joining mixed rather than single-species flocks because, while they could reduce their vigilance, they were dominant over more of the flock members and suffered less from aggression themselves.

Székely *et al.* (1989) performed a similar series of experiments to Tom Grubb's but in Oak woods near Debrecen in Hungary. In addition to the food

The supplanting attack, in which one bird
lands at the point where another is feeding,
is commonly used by Great Tits to demonstrate
dominance.

manipulations, they also altered the birds' perceived level of predation risk by flying a trained Goshawk in the woods. Like Grubb, they found that Great Tits were less likely to join mixed-species flocks when food was provided, but also that the size of such flocks was greater when the hawk was present. Furthermore, the total bird density in the wood was increased by the addition of food, and reduced by the presence of the hawk, but, again, neither food nor predator had an effect on the formation or size of single-species Great Tit flocks. Hence, they suggest that, while both food and predators may influence the participation by territory-holding Great Tits in mixed-species flocks, there may be other, non-territorial birds that continue to flock irrespective of environmental conditions. Clearly, we need to know more about the individual birds concerned in such observations to reach firmer conclusions.

Sociality and individual status

The sociality of the Great Tit has an important bearing on many aspects of its ecology and behaviour, and in particular on the degree and types (both vocal and visual) of communication that it uses. Hinde (1952) pointed out that the flocks maintained their integrity by vocalization and that a bird separated from the flock would give contact calls to try to locate it. Gompertz (1961) noted that Great Tits are not silent for long, and in describing a young male that she had hand-reared she wrote: 'it goes about its business in a nearly continuous state of exclamation'. In her study of the vocabulary of the species, she described eighteen main categories of vocalization, of which five were associated chiefly with territorial activities (not produced by females or juveniles) and four were calls given only by paired adults. An average male might have 32 distinct utterances, and one was known to have at least forty. W. Oddie (1980) advised aspiring birdwatchers that '. . . if you hear a call and you don't recognise it – it's a Great Tit'.

Some calls will be descibed later in their appropriate contexts, but here I shall briefly consider some of the commoner calls that might be heard in winter flocks. These consist largely of variations of 'tsee', 'tink', 'pink' and 'churrr' notes. The 'churrr' calls typically reflect a bird's state of alarm. Often these are prefixed by 'tsee' or 'tink' notes, which are dropped progressively as the alarm becomes more intense. Churring calls are also used when mobbing predators, and so are likely to attract the interest of other tits. The staccato 'tink' call, while used in a wide variety of contexts and repeated or not, may result in the whole flock fleeing instantly to cover. After such a response, an anxiety call 'tsee-tsui' may be given, often repeated slowly many times. After a hawk attack, the flock may remain in cover for many minutes uttering this plaintive phrase until the first bird, pressed by hunger and therefore usually a subdominant such as a yearling female, braves the risk and returns to feeding in the open (de Laet 1985a).

Clearly, social dominance and status have a considerable effect on the feeding ecology and dynamics of winter flocks. If one watches a well-stocked tit feeder in winter, one quickly becomes aware that some birds are easily and frequently supplanted or intimidated into leaving, while others stand their ground. All Great Tits are not equal. What, then, are the factors that

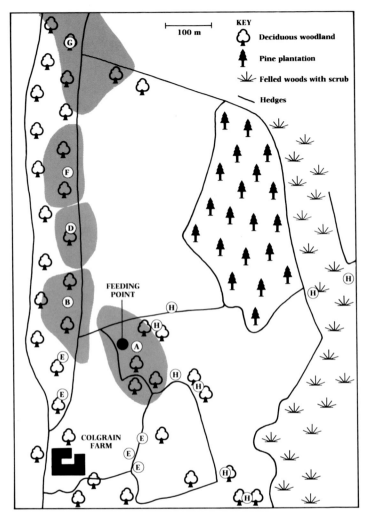

Figure 4 *Site-related dominance. The map, based on that presented by Brian (1949) shows the distribution of Great Tit territories in relation to a feeder. Territories are labelled A, B, etc. according to the dominance rank of the occupying males when interacting with others at the feeder. Hence A was dominant over B, and so on. In general, the status of a male reflected the distance to its territory. C disappeared.*

determine these differences in dominance and how do individuals recognize the status of others? Colour-ringing the birds and watching their behaviour at feeders, reveals several characteristics which repeatedly appear to determine the outcome of contests. Some of these features could be assessed visually by the birds, others only by trial and by testing an opponent's motivation to fight. Because much of this assessment is achieved visually by the use of plumage badges of dominance and posture, physical fights are actually seen rather rarely. The overriding determinant of status in Great

Tit society is the bird's sex. Males are almost invariably dominant over females (Saitou 1979b; Drent 1983) and this is true irrespective of their greater size, although (other things being equal) larger birds are more often dominant over smaller ones (Garnett 1981; Smith and Harper 1988). It has often been noted also that within each sex older birds are more likely to be senior to first-winter birds (Saitou 1979b). Such observations may, however, be biased by site-related dominance. This phenomenon, which was first described for the Great Tit by A.D. Brian (1949), occurs when an individual assumes, by virtue of its location, a status which is other than would be expected from its size and plumage. It has been observed in many populations (Drent 1983; de Laet 1984; Lemel 1989a; Sandell and Smith 1991). Brian recorded the dominance hierarchy of the tits visiting a feeder and mapped the positions of their territories relative to it. She found that birds with territories close to the feeder assumed higher status than those with distant territories (Figure 4). She also noted that a female assumed a higher status if paired with a high-ranking male if her mate was present, and Drent (1983) found that paired females assumed higher rank than unpaired ones irrespective of age. These observations show that an individual's motivation to compete is also important in determining the outcome.

The age, sex and size of an opponent can be seen, but motivation must be tested. Age is judged from the colour of the primary coverts (Chapter 1), and in this regard it is perhaps interesting that the coverts of juvenile males are often bluer than the female's. They are thus more like an adult's, although with practice one can see that they are still greener than the lesser coverts. Since the extent of greater-covert moult may indicate body condition in first-years (Gosler 1991), the number of unmoulted feathers may also act as a badge of body condition. The bird's sex is most readily judged from the width of the belly-stripe, and there is evidence that, within each sex, birds with wider stripes tend to be senior (Järvi and Bakken 1984; Smith and Harper 1988), although this again may be overridden when the resource contested is of high value – such as food during bad weather, or when contesting a territory (Smith and Harper 1988; Wilson 1992). Under such conditions, body size or motivation are more important determinants of the outcome. Probably for this reason, Brian saw no relation between stripe width and social rank. Since motivation so strongly influences dominance, one might ask why stripe size is used as a convention to settle minor disputes. Although it clearly prevents contests from escalating when the value of the contested resource is trivial, why do they use such an apparently arbitrary badge? The answer is not entirely clear, but it will almost certainly show that there is a cost to carrying a badge for seniority, which prevents individuals from wearing it if they are not also of a quality that allows them to sustain that cost. Thus, in some way, the badge must give an honest signal of the individual's fitness, so that it is not arbitrary after all (Røskaft et al. 1986; Järvi et al. 1987; Wilson 1992). Given the apparent importance of plumage marks in settling disputes, it is not surprising that postures have evolved that exaggerate those features at such times. In the next chapter, we shall continue this theme by considering the defence of a resource of great importance: the territory.

6

TERRITORY AND SONG: FORM AND FUNCTION

IN the last chapter, I described flocking as one end of a spectrum of social behaviour from full sociability to semi-isolation. The other end of this spectrum results from territoriality, i.e., when a male or pair establishes an area as its own and excludes all other Great Tits from it. These territories may range in size from about 0.2 to 4 ha, depending on density, and the pressure from neighbours (Krebs 1977a), and on the age of the male. Older males tend to occupy larger (Krebs 1971; Dhondt 1971a) and, in some sites, also better-quality territories (Dhondt and Hublé 1968a). How does this arise if, as we have seen, males rarely change territories between years? Dhondt (1971a) showed that it came about because the survival rate of young males on better territories was greater than for those on poor ones, so that there was effectively selection for males on better territories. The fact that there may be unoccupied ground of (apparently) suitable habitat between territories (Hinde 1952) suggests that there are constraints on the size of area that can be defended, for a territory must be won. If population density is low, this may involve a young male simply declaring a free area to be his. If the density is high, it may involve physical combat. Either way, once established, the incumbent, needs only to restate his presence regularly for his boundaries to be maintained and respected. This is of course an oversimplification because, while neighbours respect each other's boundaries once tested, incursions from first-year hopefuls must still be discouraged. Although site-related dominance usually makes this simple, a few aspiring 'landowners' may be more persistent so a contest may escalate from simple display to full combat. From the vigour with which territories are defended and the fact that few non-territorial pairs breed successfully, we must assume that the possession of a territory is of the utmost importance to them, so we should first ask why this is so.

Territory

There are two main ideas concerning the function of territory. These are not mutually exclusive. The first suggests that the pair must secure an area free from competitors to provide enough food for the growing brood. This could be particularly important for the birds to forage optimally (Chapter 3), since it may be easier to monitor the average patch quality if only the pair members themselves are responsible for the depletion of those patches. The second suggestion is that there may be some benefit to the breeding pair in distancing themselves from neighbours. This refers to the fact that territoriality results in an average spacing between nests which is greater than expected from a random distribution, a condition described as 'over-dispersed' (Krebs 1971). This benefit could arise either from a reduced risk of nest predation by Weasels or from a reduction in the level of interference that the pair suffers during the breeding season. The predation argument points out that, since predators such as Weasels are themselves territorial, if each predator has fewer tit nests within its territory, it is less likely to develop the skills needed to specialize on tit broods. There are three lines of evidence that support this idea. First, pairs on small territories fledge fewer young than do those with larger territories, and this is largely because they are more likely to lose their clutch or brood to a predator (McCleery and Perrins 1985). Second, the risk of Weasel predation depends on the density of tit nests (Krebs 1970). Third, Weasels prefer to eat small mammals, and switch to raiding tit nests only when small-mammal numbers are low (Dunn 1977); this suggests that they might indeed need to develop different skills to take tits.

There is also strong evidence supporting the interference idea, which argues that, although Great Tits are strictly monogamous, males should still space themselves so as to reduce the risk of their partner mating with a neighbouring male during the short period when she is forming eggs (Møller 1990). This may be a risk, because if a female has paired with a male of poor quality it might be in her best interests (in terms of the quality of chicks produced) to mate with another male if he is of higher quality than her own. If such an 'extra-pair copulation' (EPC) resulted in an 'extra-pair fertilization' (EPF), it would later result in a male unwittingly wasting energy raising another male's chick. Three observations support this idea also. First, Norris and Blakey (1989) presented evidence that cuckoldry did occur. Second, much of the male's time and energy is spent guarding his mate during her fertile period, especially early in the morning when most copulations occur (Björklund and Westman 1986; Mace 1986, 1987a, 1987b). Third, Møller (1990) drew attention to Hinde's observation that territory size is at its greatest during the female's fertile period. Björklund *et al.* (1992) showed that the presence of a male on his territory reduced the likelihood of incursion, but even if he was temporarily removed females rejected 95 per cent of advances made by intruders. This is perhaps not surprising since, on average, many intruding males will be of poorer quality than her own, she cannot necessarily assess the genetic quality of a male from outward appearances, and because the contribution that her mate will later make to feeding the brood is essential to her breeding success, so that she cannot afford to risk losing his 'confidence' that the chicks are his.

The male's presence is announced by song. Females will sing (although poorly) if they need to contact their partner quickly. There is no doubt that male song serves the purpose of territorial advertisement, although its involvement in pair formation (its other suggested role) is debatable. John Krebs (1977a, 1982) ran a series of experiments over several years in which he temporarily removed territorial males in early spring from a small wood. If he then played recorded Great Tit song in the vacant territories, these took nearly three times as long to be reoccupied by new birds than if he did nothing. Territories with no deterrence were refilled within eight hours. He also found that colonization of the area where song was played occurred gradually by encroachment from the sides, while the area without song was reoccupied simultaneously by several birds. Furthermore, the response of an intruder to recorded song depended on how long it had been within the unoccupied area. If this had been only a short time, the bird was more likely to retreat than if it had been present for longer. If he then reintroduced the original territory-holder, a contest ensued that escalated faster and further, from display to full combat, than would normally occur between neighbours or established territory-holders and intruders. The chances of the original occupant regaining his ground were directly related to the length of time that the new arrival had been on territory. After a few days, only about 10 per cent of males were able to regain their territories. The period of occupancy was far more important in determining the result of such contests than qualitative differences between the birds such as their relative ages or sizes. Krebs (1982) described such a contest as a war of attrition in which short bouts of display and attack were punctuated by breaks in which either party had the chance to retreat. In such a situation, the potential cost of a protracted contest to the new bird gradually declines relative to the cost to the original owner as the duration of the new bird's occupancy increases. Through the unexpectedly strong motivation of the new occupant to contest the issue, the original owner comes to recognize that he is now an intruder and runs the risk of injury. He therefore retreats.

Territorial contests consist of bouts of song and display. Three displays in particular are seen. Two of these are also used in the flock or at a feeder as intimidation. In the first, which Brian (1949) termed 'pointing', the bird adopts a vertical posture with bill pointing skywards. This clearly displays the belly-stripe. The wings are held close to the body, the feathers sleeked and the tail spread little or not at all. The body may rotate from side to side to enhance the effect further. The second posture is clearly more imminently

A male Great Tit advertises his territorial boundaries by the use of song. Great Tit song contains much information about the character and motivation of the singer.

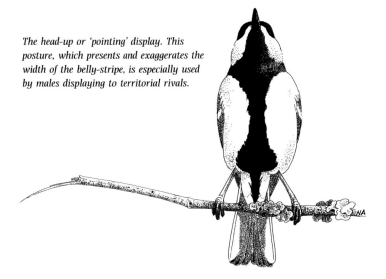

The head-up or 'pointing' display. This posture, which presents and exaggerates the width of the belly-stripe, is especially used by males displaying to territorial rivals.

threatening. In this, the body is held horizontally, the belly-stripe is not displayed, the wings and tail are spread and the feathers slightly fluffed, and the bill (the main weapon), which may be opened slightly, points directly at the opponent. While the first posture emphasizes the size of the belly-stripe relative to the body, the latter increases the apparent size of the bird, so the displays differ in context. The former is rarely used to threaten other species; the latter frequently is. The third display is a development of the first and is not used to dispute food. In this, one male flies vertically in a series of short, flicks around his opponent, but retains the vertical posture. This strange display could be called a 'pointing flight'. If the opponent retaliates, a towering fight may ensue. Although the horizontal threat is used by any individual, pointing and pointing flights are more often employed by males.

Although many of the new birds that arrived when Krebs removed territory-holders were first-years from poor hedgerow territories nearby, some were adults. Furthermore, some arrived already paired, suggesting that territory might not be necessary to obtain a mate. In this they resembled the Belgian guest pairs described on page 48. The reason why a male does not normally change his territory once he has bred there is probably that moving to an area of unknown quality is more risky than staying in a poor territory he has learned to exploit. Older males tend to breed more successfully than first-timers, and this is probably because of acquired experience. Indeed, experienced birds breeding together for the first time are less successful than established pairs of the same age (Perrins and McCleery 1985). Although pair formation may occur within winter flocks, it is generally agreed that females select males from among the territory-holders available in spring. This is supported by the fact that, when divorces occur, it is the females rather than the males that change territory, suggesting that they were responsible. But what qualities should a female look for when choosing a mate? Ultimately, they should be those which will give her the greatest opportunity to raise healthy chicks that stand a chance of being

The forward-threat display, in which the bill (the main weapon) is aimed at a rival, is used by any Great Tit to threaten others of the same or other species.

recruited next year to the breeding population. But how can she know? Are the qualities of the male more important than those of his territory or vice versa, or are they correlated so that good males have good territories? In such a case, a selection for one would be a selection for the other also.

Forming pairs

We know rather little about the process of pair formation in the Great Tit, or the criteria that the female uses to make her choice, but there is some evidence that females select males rather than their territories (as suggested above). Norris (1990a, 1990b) found that in Marley Wood the breeding performance of a male was unrelated to the quality of his territory, but was related to the width of his belly-stripe. Males with large stripes were more attentive to the brood, which therefore received more food, grew faster and were heavier at fledging. This greater attentiveness also increased the chance that a predator at the nest would be detected and attacked. In some years, such males were also more likely to pair with females that laid larger and earlier clutches. Furthermore, a divorced female that had previously laid a large clutch was more likely to re-pair with a large-striped male. Hence, Norris suggests that females should choose males with large belly-stripes because they are more likely to make good fathers. However, plumage might not be the only criterion used. Lindén (1990) found that pairs were more likely to divorce after a poor breeding season, suggesting that divorce was an attempt (assumed to be by the female) to improve future breeding success. Greenwood *et al.* (1979a) found that older females that divorced after breeding with a first-year male were more likely to pair with an older male the next year. Although the evidence that females generally prefer older males is poor, there are good reasons why they should. First, they are more likely to breed successfully with an older male than a first-year male (Perrins and McCleery 1985). Second, whatever the characteristics determining a bird's chances of survival, an older bird has proved that he has what it takes. Hence, if those traits are genetically determined, they are likely to be inherited by her offspring if she pairs with him. It should be added that the width of a male's belly-stripe does not vary with age (Wilson 1992).

Clearly, many factors could influence a female's choice of mate if there are enough unpaired males in the population to offer a choice. But what of the male's song? Although the function of song in territory defence is proven in the denser European populations, Björklund *et al.* (1989) found that, in an area of Sweden that was more sparsely populated by tits and where the birds were fully migratory, pairing occurred only after territory establishment, most of the tits needed to find new partners each year, males sang less synchronously than they should if singing only to defend a territory and they reduced their song output by 50 per cent once paired. Hence, it was suggested, song was more significant to the pairing process than to territory defence. In Britain also, Krebs *et al.* (1981a) found that males, if their mate was removed, greatly increased the amount of time that they spent singing, but the quality of the song did not change. New partners were usually found quickly. If qualities of a male's song other than simply its total output are involved in pair formation, we should ask what information does song convey. To do this, we need to look at the nature of Great Tit song and how it varies between males.

The 'pointing' flight is an exaggerated development of the pointing display, and therefore occurs in escalated contests between males.

Song and its functions

The song of the Great Tit in Europe has been described as 'tea-cher, tea-cher, tea-cher', with the sound quality of a squeaky bicycle pump. Asian Great Tits sing quite differently from those in Europe (Hailman 1989), and indeed their songs are unrecognizable to European Great Tits (Gompertz 1968). Although 'tea-cher, tea-cher' allows recognition of the species, there is much variation on this theme in Europe. Once again I must restrict this discussion to Europe because, although much work on song has been done here, there has been little elsewhere. Great Tits sing songs at a frequency of between about 4–6.5 kHz. A song consists of a series of two to six notes ('tea' and 'cher' are notes) repeated several times to form a phrase or 'strophe' ('tea-cher, tea-cher, tea-cher' is a strophe). Songs are produced in bursts consisting of several such strophes punctuated by periods of silence. The bird may then change song type. Each male may have as many as eight distinct song types (mostly two to four), classified by the number of notes in a strophe, the ways in which frequency and amplitude change over time and the time taken to repeat a strophe (McGregor and Krebs 1982b). A population such as that at Marley Wood, Wytham, may have more than forty song types in any year, and no song type is any more commonly produced than any other in the population as a whole. Furthermore, over time there is no consistency in the songs produced in a particular area or territory, so that the song types present in the population gradually change over the years. The rate at which songs change in a population is related to the survival rate of its members (McGregor and Krebs 1989). Males differ in the numbers and types of song that they sing, and share more song types with neighbouring territory-holders than with more distant males (McGregor and Krebs 1982b). The number of songs a male sings constitutes his 'repertoire size'. In addition to repertoire size and strophe length, which are consistent for a given male, males differ in the degree to which they can produce strophes consistently. A change in the duration of pauses between strophes over time is termed 'drift' (Lambrechts and Dhondt 1987). A great deal of experimental work has been carried out, mostly in the field, to discover why these birds sing in such a way, and this must necessarily be a brief introduction to a fascinating story.

The pattern of song production through a population arises from the way in which songs are learned. Males learn some common song types before they are fully independent, but others are learned from neighbours once a territory has been established. There may, therefore, be little similarity between a male's songs and those of his father or other relatives, but songs are shared between territorial neighbours (McGregor and Krebs 1982b). Furthermore, songs can be learned throughout life, but, although the song-types produced by a male may change with time as his neighbours change, they tend to replace songs previously produced. Hence, a male's repertoire size may increase little with age (McGregor and Krebs 1989), although it seems that populations differ in the degree to which this is so (Lambrechts and Dhondt 1986). One effect of all this is that Great Tit males recognize more songs than they produce (McGregor and Avery 1986).

This pattern of learning and replacement is functional, because songs are usually produced in alternating bouts of duetting whereby a male sings the same song in response to a neighbour. This 'song-matching' has the obvious advantage that it allows the male to indicate 'I am answering you, and to prove it this is what you last said'. It is perhaps this precision that makes males with larger repertoires better at deterring intruders (Krebs *et al.* 1978b). Song-matching, however, has another function: if a receiving male knows what song to expect, and knows what it should sound like, then the degree to which what is actually received differs from that expected sound (its degradation) can be used to judge the transmitter's distance (Krebs *et al.* 1981b; McGregor *at al.* 1983; McGregor and Krebs 1984). Such a use of song must take account of differences in the habitat through which the sounds must travel. In this regard, it is interesting that Hunter and Krebs (1979) found that across ten sites through Europe, from England to Iran, songs differed in structure more in relation to habitat than in relation to geographical separation. In particular, the songs of Great Tits in dense forest vegetation in Sweden, Norway, England, Poland and Morocco were more similar to each other than they were to those produced by birds in more open woodland in England, Spain, Greece, Iran and Morocco. Similarly, woodland songs recorded hundreds of kilometres apart resembled each other more than they did forest songs recorded just a few kilometres away. Forest songs had lower maximum frequencies, a narrower frequency range and fewer notes per strophe than woodland songs, and it was found that this could be explained by the fact that frequencies above 5.6 kHz were more rapidly lost in the denser forest habitats. On average, the maximum frequency produced in woodland was 6.5 kHz.

Clearly, the structure of Great Tit song is adaptive, but why do woodland males have large repertories? There have been several suggestions, and most have some supporting evidence. The first is that birds may tire of listening to the same song and come to ignore it. Krebs (1976) found that Great Tits do indeed become habituated in this way to some extent. Song-switching would reduce the likelihood of this. In dense populations, as we have already seen, a repertoire allows an individual to indicate for whom a song is intended. Krebs (1976, 1977b) suggested that perhaps a male with many songs could use this to give the impression that the density of birds in a particular area was higher than it really was, which would imply to an intruder that its breeding success would be low if it were to settle there (Chapter 4). If this 'Beau Geste' hypothesis were correct, however, one would expect males to deliver different songs from different perches, and this does not happen (Lambrechts and Dhondt 1988b, Björklund *et al.* 1989). The most important question is whether or not males with larger repertoires are fitter individuals. There is now much to suggest that this is so. McGregor *et al.* (1981) found that males who sang more songs had a greater chance of breeding in the following year, and produced more young, more heavy young and, most importantly, more recruits than birds with smaller repertoires. Lambrechts and Dhondt (1986) found that Belgian male Great Tits with large repertoires also sang longer strophes and showed less drift in their songs, and again that such males were more likely to survive to the following year and to breed more successfully. In addition, good singers tended to be socially dominant at a feeder irrespective of the distance from their territory, although it is interesting that Lambrechts and Dhondt (1988a) found no relationship between these measures of song quality and territory quality.

How do these characteristics indicate a male's quality? Lambrechts and Dhondt (1988b) suggested that singing was an exhausting business and that only good-quality males could produce songs with long strophes, and little drift. They argued that strophe length indicated the bird's resistance to fatigue and that, independently of this, song-switching might allow the use of different muscles and so reduce strain. Weary *et al.* (1988) suggested that motivation must be important in determining song production and that drift could result from changes in motivation while singing. After some debate and further experimentation, it seems that both may be valid explanations for variations in Great Tit song production, but that further work is required (Weary *et al.* 1991; McGregor and Horn 1992).

So, what do female Great Tits think of all this? Although, as we have seen, there is much to suggest that they should prefer to mate with males who have large repertoires, Krebs *et al.* (1978b) have argued that there is little evidence for this. They found that females paired with such males were not able to lay any earlier or to lay larger clutches than other females. This is perhaps not surprising, since males do not influence the number of eggs laid by their partners,and we have seen that territory quality (which might affect these things) is rarely related to male quality. Lambrechts (1992) treated captive female Great Tits with harmless subcutaneous implants of a female hormone. This heightens the female's interest in male stimuli, so that she adopts a copulation-solitication posture if aroused. He found that these females actually seemed to prefer songs with short strophes, showing that any relationship between song quality and mate selection cannot be straightforward. In a similar procedure, Baker *et al.* (1987) found that females from Wytham responded more to the songs of Wytham males than to those recorded in parkland a few kilometres away. This complemented McGregor and Krebs's (1982b) observation that Wytham females were more likely to pair with males whose songs were similar to, but not the same as, their father's. Greenwood *et al.* (1979a) also found that Wytham residents were more likely to pair with other residents than expected by chance. This suggests that females take an interest in the male's songs, but perhaps they use them in some way to assess how closely related they are. This may be important, because chicks from related parents are less likely to survive owing to genetic difficulties (Bulmer 1973; Greenwood *et al.* 1978). Despite this, in the island population of Vlieland, where opportunities for pairing with an immigrant are reduced, there is strong genetic evidence that females are not influenced by genetic relatedness in their selection of a mate (Van Noordwijk and Scharloo 1981; Van Noordwijk *et al.* 1985, 1988). It would seem, then, that populations must differ in the ways in which males use song and in the ways that females interpret or respond to those songs, and whether females use song at all to assess male quality remains unclear.

7

THE BREEDING SEASON: NEST-BUILDING TO HATCHING

MANY activities described in the last two chapters have evolved to result in a stable pair on a defined breeding territory, with the female ready to lay her first egg around the middle of April. The exact time differs between years and varies between geographical regions and between territories within a population. Much preparation must take place before the female can commit herself by starting the clutch, because, as we shall see, timing is everything to the success of this venture and she must make all the important decisions in this regard.

The first outwardly visible sign of the start of the breeding season is nest-building. In a hole, selected by the female from several presented by the male for inspection, the female constructs the nest. She may have roosted in this nest hole for some days or weeks before building begins. Perhaps this gives her the opportunity to assess its suitability more fully, since there will be much at stake later if her selection is poor. The foundation, which may be 5 cm deep, is typically of moss pressed flat by a rubbing action of the female's belly. The quantity of moss that this small bird must collect can be staggering, for she fills the floor area of the cavity to the same depth even if this is more than 30 cm in diameter. The male takes no part in nest-building, although he may accompany her when she is collecting material, and indeed Perrins (1979) points out that the female is dominant over him at the nest site. The moss foundation is usually topped and lined with hair or fur, but rarely with feathers as is the case with the Blue Tit. In this foundation a cup-shaped depression is formed by the same rubbing action used to compress the moss. Early in the season, a nest may appear to take more than a week to complete, but clearly this is not necessary since later in the season when time is short an adequate nest can be constructed in a day.

The Great Tit's breeding season in Oak woodland is timed so that the period of the eventual brood's greatest demand coincides with the peak abundance of caterpillars such as those of the Winter Moth, although the peak date differs from year to year depending largely on the spring temperature. It is not surprising, then, that the date a clutch is started is closely related to the temperature in March or April, being earlier in a warm spring (Perrins 1965; Orell and Ojanen 1983a; Perrins and McCleery 1989). If the tits timed their laying by the temperature directly, however, even this level of control would sometimes be inadequate to match the brood to the available food. This is because if the caterpillars hatched early relative to the bud burst (their own food supply) many would die, leaving little food for the tits. Hence, Perrins (1991) has suggested that the relationship between laying date and temperature reflects the tits tracking the availability of caterpillars rather than the temperature itself (but *see* Nager 1990).

Once the clutch is started, there are limits to the options available for fine-tuning the date of hatching in accordance with the developing season. It is generally easier for her to delay hatching than to bring it forward. For example, since one egg is laid each day until the clutch is complete, she might skip a day during laying (although this is less common in the Great Tit than in other tits) or she can elect not to start incubation immediately after laying the last egg. The longest such delay that I have encountered in which the brood hatched successfully was eight days, but this was exceptional and delays of more than two days are rare. Alternatively, the female can bring the hatch forward by starting to incubate up to three days before the clutch is complete. This, however, results in the last egg(s) hatching after the rest (Haftorn 1981a). Such hatching asynchrony results in a spread in chick ages, and the smaller chicks will not survive in competition with their older siblings unless food is abundant. Actions to delay hatching are most often seen in early nests, while later breeding attempts more often show strategies that bring the hatch forward.

The female can also control the timing by adjusting the number of eggs she lays, but here there are other considerations. Since an egg takes four days to develop before laying, the decision to start it must be made some days before it is laid, although unlaid eggs can be resorbed. Once incubation starts, the course is more or less set for that brood, because there is less that she can do to alter the growth rate of the embryos and they will die if they become chilled. Food for the brood is not the only consideration in her timing, since early-fledged chicks have an advantage when they in turn come to compete for food and territories later in the year. It must be remembered that the parents' goal is not just to fledge a few chicks, but to have as many as possible recruited into the breeding population. There may thus be a conflict between the need to fledge chicks early (which may also allow the parents to start a second brood) and the availability of food.

Laying and clutch size

The female roosts on the nest during the laying period. Although she is in partial contact with the eggs, they do not receive enough heat from her to start their development. The day's egg is laid early in the morning, before the male arrives and calls her out with a distinctive note that Kluijver (1950) described as sounding like 'saw-sharpening'. Kluijver described the female's responding call as a 'soft whining sound'. The male has spent the night in another hole in the territory. Male song early in the morning at this time is associated with intense mate-guarding, for it is important for him to be seen to be present now to prevent incursions by neighbours (Björklund and Westman 1986; Mace 1986, 1987a, 1987b). This implies that neighbours or unpaired males are aware of the stage in breeding that the pair has reached, since the female is receptive only during the laying period. The pair members spend much time together during the day at this stage, the female

Egg variation in the Great Tit. While eggs from different clutches vary greatly in colour, there is little variation within clutches. Egg patterning varies in the size, density and intensity of spotting. Compare the fine, light spotting of the clutch above with the heavy, dark speckling of that below. We do not, as yet, understand the significance of these differences.

'Courtship feeding' has little to do with courtship since the pair is well established by the time that it occurs. Rather, the extra food provided by the male is essential to help the female to produce eggs.

receiving perhaps a third of her food from the male. During this so-called 'courtship-feeding' (which has nothing to do with courtship), the female begs like a fledgling for food from the male, while giving a distinctive squeaky call described by Gompertz (1961) as 'zeedle-zeedle-zeedle-zee' and therefore called 'zeedling'. During copulation, the male 'zeedles' also.

Courtship-feeding is almost certainly necessary for the female to produce a clutch (Royama 1966). In northern populations, Great Tit eggs weigh between 1.3 and 2.3 g. This is often more than 10 per cent of the female's weight so that the full clutch of four to twelve eggs may weigh more than she does. About 6 per cent of the egg weight is in the shell, but, of the contents, some 81.5 per cent is water. Of the remaining dry matter within the egg, some 43 per cent is protein and 33 per cent fats (pers. comm. J.C. Yoo). Summed over a clutch of ten with a mean weight of 1.7 g, this is about

1.3 g of protein and 1 g of fat in addition to the extra calcium and water. It is doubtful that the female alone could meet these requirements. That food for the laying female is limited is suggested by the fact that eggs tend to be heavier when the temperature over the four-day development period prior to laying is higher (Jones 1973), and that eggs in replacement and second clutches are usually heavier than those of her first clutch (Perrins 1970) the former are laid later, when caterpillars are larger and more abundant.

Like the timing of laying, the decision as to the size of clutch must take account of several factors. It may seem at first sight that the female should simply lay as large a clutch as she can to increase the chance of having young recruited. Since females readily start a replacement clutch if their first clutch is lost, it is clear that they could often lay more eggs than they do. Large clutches produce large broods, and these naturally require more food than a smaller one. Since there is a ceiling to the rate at which a pair can bring food to the nest, each chick in a large brood tends to receive less food than if there were fewer young, hence they fledge at a lighter weight than chicks from smaller broods (Perrins 1965). This is important, because light fledglings are less likely to survive to the winter. There is therefore a trade-off that the female must make between the quantity and quality of chicks that she produces later as a result of the size of clutch she lays now.

We should expect evolution to adapt birds to lay the clutch size which gives the greatest number of recruits per brood, i.e., the commonest clutch size in the population should be the most productive (Lack 1954), but this is not so. Although close to it, in several populations studied, females lay a clutch about one egg smaller than the observed optimum. Several reasons have been put forward for this, but three in particular have come to the fore in recent years. The first suggests that different habitats may differ in their most productive clutch sizes: hence, immigration of females adapted to a poorer habitat such as hedgerows, where the most productive clutch might be lower, would result in a reduction in the average clutch size laid by the population (Perrins 1990a). This 'gene-flow' argument is compelling but on the face of it, suffers from the fact that, in Wytham at least (where the mean clutch size is below the most productive), immigrant females do not lay smaller clutches than residents (McCleery and Clobert 1990). Hence, immigrants are not seen to reduce the average clutch size of the population as might be expected. However, the gene-flow idea could still be correct if the dispersal of a bird in or out of the population was in some way related to the clutch size from which it came. Furthermore, evidence in support of it has come from patchy Mediterranean habitats (Blondel et al. 1987) and from Belgium, where poorer habitats do indeed appear to have lower optimum clutch sizes (Dhondt et al. 1990). Clearly, further work in this area is needed.

The second idea has become known as the 'trade-off hypothesis'. This has received somewhat wavering support in recent years. It suggests that if there is a cost to a female in terms of her own survival incurred by producing a larger clutch, perhaps she balances (or trades off) the value of the current brood (value to her lifetime reproductive success) against the value of future broods. That is, by reducing the number of chicks produced this year, she may increase the likelihood that she will survive to breed next year. However, the probability of a female Great Tit surviving to breed in the following year seems unrelated to the size of the current year's brood (Boer-Hazewinkel 1987; Pettifor et al. 1988; McCleery and Clobert 1990). Although this year's brood is not traded off against next year's, this does not mean that, in those populations where second broods occur, the value of an early brood cannot be weighed against that of a second brood in the same season. By swapping chicks between nests, Smith et al. (1987, 1989) and Tinbergen (1987) changed the size of first broods that Swedish and Dutch Great Tits raised. They found that, although raising a large brood did not affect the physical condition of the parents, it did reduce the likelihood of their producing a second clutch. This was because enlarged broods stayed in the nest for longer than small broods, so that parents had less time available to raise another brood; and because the delay also reduced the value of second broods, since later-fledged young compete less well for food and are therefore less likely to be recruited. Slagsvold (1984) suggested that, if predation of first clutches was intense, it might pay birds to lay a smaller first clutch, which could be reared more quickly and with a guarantee of producing more young from a second brood.

The third idea concerning the discrepancy between the most common and the most productive clutch sizes is known as the 'individual optimization hypothesis' (Pettifor et al. 1988). This suggests that females lay that size of clutch and hence produce that brood which they (and their mate) can best raise given the prevailing conditions of food supply and date. Like Smith et al., Pettifor manipulated the sizes of broods that parent Great Tits had to raise. He consistently found that the best brood size (that yielding the greatest number of recruits per brood) was that which corresponded to the size of clutch that the female originally laid. Birds raising enlarged or reduced broods usually had fewer young recruited than those raising unaltered broods. This in fact suggests that the females do lay the size of clutch which yields the greatest number of recruits per brood, but the best clutch size for a particular pair is less than the best for the whole population. How is this possible? Suppose that the average recruitment rate for birds raising their optimum is 40 per cent. Clearly, a pair with ten young (four recruits) will have more young recruited than a pair raising five (two recruits). But suppose that the recruitment rate of the pair raising five young fell to only 10 per cent if they were to attempt to raise ten, they would then manage to have only one chick recruited. Clearly, it would have been better for *them* to have had a smaller brood even if, overall, those that were able to raise a larger brood produced more recruits. This is remarkable because the best brood size for a pair must depend partly on the abilities of the male, and for many females this cannot have been tested. It is probably for this reason that pairs that have bred together previously are more successful than newly formed pairs of birds of similar age (Perrins and McCleery 1985). Slagsvold and Lifjeld (1990) showed that female Great Tits were able to adjust their clutch size in relation to their own abilities, but were not able so to compensate for such failings in the male.

Clearly, many factors influence the female in deciding how many eggs to lay, and these must be responsible for the variation in clutch sizes that is observed. In most populations, earlier clutches are larger than later ones, replacement clutches are usually smaller than first clutches and second clutches smaller still. That this reduction occurs while food availability is improving suggests that the birds follow a strategy related to the number of chicks that can be raised, rather than being limited by the food supply. The average clutch tends to be smaller in later seasons, or in poorer habitats, if laid by a first-year female, if in a smaller cavity, or when the population density is high, but this is not always so (Perrins and McCleery 1989) and indeed the strength of many of these relationships may differ markedly between populations (Van Noordwijk et al. 1981). Although the effect of cavity size may be an adaptation to reduce heat stress in the chicks (it is not because there is insufficient space in the nest for more eggs; Van Balen and Cavé 1970; Van Balen 1984), the other effects are probably related to the food supply, for clutch size also varies between years according to the abundance of caterpillars (Perrins and McCleery 1989; Perrins 1990b). It is curious that the caterpillar density does not also affect when the female starts her clutch, because this *can* be hastened by providing the birds with extra food. This is all the more strange because such artificial provisioning does not affect her clutch size (Källander 1974; Perrins 1991). How the tits manage all this is still the subject of intense research and debate, but results so far suggest that they may use insects from the shrub layer (in which they feed early in the season) to form eggs, and those from the tree canopy later to provision the brood (pers. comm. T. Achiron-Frumkin).

The eggs

Apart from their greater size, Great Tit eggs are much like those of other tits (and also those of Nuthatches and Treecreepers) in that they are glossy white with a variable scattering of reddish or brown spots. The spots tend to be concentrated at the blunt end but may cover the whole surface; they also vary in intensity, from very pale to very dark red. A few eggs (less than 5 per cent) are pure white, sometimes with just one or two small black spots as if the pigment had been compressed into the area of a pinhead. Although it has not been tested formally, egg colour appears to be constant for a particular female, as are her egg size, clutch size and laying date relative to the rest of the population (Van Noordwijk 1987): Eggs within a clutch clearly resemble each other more than they do eggs of other clutches (page 71). At present we have no idea what function these pigments serve, if indeed there is any. Certainly it is not for camouflage. During incubation, Great Tit eggs decline in weight by about 16 per cent owing to water loss, and this also does not seem to be influenced by the intensity or distribution of pigment (J.C. Yoo pers. comm.). Gibb (1970) noticed that if he numbered the eggs, the female had usually turned them over by the next time he visited, so the number was not showing. It is difficult to analyse statistically whether this could occur by chance, because the eggs must be turned regularly during incubation to ensure an even warming. There is, however, at least the suggestion that the female takes some interest in the appearance of the eggs, although she will not reject additional eggs placed in the nest.

Incubation

After laying, the female usually covers the eggs with nest lining, but uncovers them when she returns to roost in the evening. Haftorn (1981a) suggests that the transition from this behaviour to full incubation is rather more gradual than might be supposed, since some incubation occurs every night that the female is at roost, although it may be for only half an hour. A few days before the last egg is laid, her brood-patch is fully developed. This is a bare area of the belly, which becomes inflamed with blood vessels and is hot to the touch. If the female chooses to incubate the clutch fully before its completion to hasten their hatching, she needs only to spend more time in full contact with the eggs at night. For reasons already discussed, this occurs more frequently in later than in early clutches. Slagsvold and Amundsen (1992), however, have suggested that earlier nesters might follow a similar strategy if they could, but that they are prevented from doing so by the amount of food available for the incubating female. Full daytime incubation develops about two to three days after full nocturnal incubation (Haftorn 1981a) and lasts about thirteen days. During this time, the female maintains the egg-surface temperature close to 35.4 °C by alternating periods of about half an hour on with ten minutes off, depending on air temperature. A long period off will be followed by a longer period on. The total incubation time is about 320–400 hours, being shorter if she spends more time on, and longer if she must spend more time off to feed. The incubation time is also shorter if the egg temperature is maintained closer to 36 °C and longer if it is cooler (Haftorn 1981b, 1983). All this means that the female may get only three hours each day to feed, so that food provided by the male is probably as important at this time as when forming the eggs. Kluijver (1950) found that, on average, males visited the nest 6.9 times per hour with food for the incubating female, although the rate varied through the day, being as high as 26 times per hour in the morning or as few as once per hour in the afternoon.

As in the other *Parus* tits, incubation is undertaken entirely by the female. If she is disturbed at the nest during this, she will often defend her clutch by a distinctive threat display in which she spreads the tail, flicks the wings against the sides of the nest cavity and emits a loud hissing call. It is possible that in the dark cavity this may sound sufficiently like a snake to dissuade a predatory mammal such as a Weasel from entering the nest, but its effectiveness in this regard has not been tested. The female also faces the entrance to the chamber more often than not, and this presumably gives her more chance to detect the approach of a predator and to leave more quickly if she wishes. Despite this, incubating birds sometimes sit tight on the nest when disturbed (page 11), preferring even to be gently pushed aside for inspection of the clutch rather than to leave the nest entirely; nevertheless, they should not be handled more than this as this increases the risk that they will desert the clutch.

8

THE BREEDING SEASON: HATCHING TO FLEDGING

WITH the hatching of the first chick, Great Tit parents enter the most intensely active period of their year. If singing and territorial defence were exhausting, these activities are surely nothing compared with what is to come, for during the next 18–21 days the pair may deliver more than 10,000 caterpillars to the nest. Furthermore, since they will rarely bring more than one prey item at a time, the parents must also make almost this number of round trips to the nest. Over the whole nestling period, this is equivalent to a total flight distance of at least 100 km for each of them. During the period of peak demand, when the brood is about seven to ten days old, they may return to the nest every ninety seconds with prey. It is perhaps difficult to conceive just how great a feat this is. Kluijver (1950) observed that each nestling in a Great Tit brood of ten received some 64 g of prey (fresh weight) during their twenty days in the nest. For the whole brood, then, this represents a total of about 640 g. For the parents, this is equivalent to delivering about seventeen times their own combined body weights in food to the brood during the course of just three weeks. If translated directly into human terms, this would be something like a couple bringing home 103 kg (227 lb) of shopping every day for three weeks! Fortunately for the birds, such a comparison is not really valid because of differences in the effects of scale, but, nonetheless, there can be little doubt that this must be a stressful time for the tits.

Under such a regime it would not be surprising to find that the parents lost weight during this time, and to some extent this is this case. Females lose a considerable amount of weight during the nestling period. Rheinwald (1981) found that, in Germany, seven female Great Tits lost 0.13 g per day on average during this time. Most of this weight loss, however, is due to a reduction in the size of tissues that have become greatly enlarged before egg-laying, such as the ovary, oviduct and brood-patch; in this latter case, reduction in size leaves the skin loose and wrinkled on the belly. Rheinwald also found that little of the weight loss was due to the use of fat reserves and in fact, despite the rigours of chick-rearing, both parents are able to build up a fat store in a remarkably predictable manner each day for use overnight (Gosler 1991). However, some of the weight loss is due to a reduction in the size of the pectoral muscles, which suggests a net loss of protein, in turn supporting the view that the birds are stressed. Surprisingly, males do not show such weight or muscle reduction during the nestling period, and in fact they may even increase in weight during it (Gosler 1991).

It takes a remarkable feat of endurance to produce a brood of Great Tits, because the chicks' rate of growth and development is no less remarkable. For a brood of ten, 64 g of prey turns each chick from a blind, naked hatchling weighing about 1.3 g into a fully feathered fledgling, eyes open, and, at about fifteen times the hatchling weight, all set to take its first flight (p. 87). At hatching, the chick is little more than a machine for turning insect protein into Great Tit. Much of its weight is made up by the gut. Despite their size, the tiny legs provide some support, for the chick, as soon as it has broken free of the egg, responds to the returning parent by begging for food in the manner characteristic of all baby passerines. The disproportionately large head provides for a disproportionately large gape to serve as an adequate target for the parent upon its return, because prey are forcefully inserted into the gaping mouths of the chicks. Figures 5a and 5b (overleaf) show the average growth in weight, wing and tarsus lengths, bill length and depth and width of gape flange of Great Tit chicks at Wytham during the first fifteen days. Note that by this age the tarsus is fully grown and the weight has reached a plateau, the width of the gape has already peaked and is now decreasing, the bill depth is about three-quarters of its final size, while the bill and wing lengths are only about two-thirds of their final dimensions. These last three features will not be fully grown until up

Naked and blind, the tiny hatchlings, which weigh only about 1.3 g, beg for food as soon as they are free of the shell.

Bill-wiping, in which the bill is drawn from its base to its tip along the perch, is used especially in the spring to hone the bill. This may adapt the bill better for feeding on insects.

to two weeks after fledging, but notice that at its peak growth rate (where the curve of Figure 5a is steepest), between days eight and nine, the wing length increases by a full centimetre. Gibb (1950) noted that the age at which events such as the development of the feathers occurred was independent of a chick's weight, so that these could be used as a guide to its age (although this would not be true if the chick were severely under-nourished, perhaps owing to the loss of a parent, or the habitat being poor).

Although they average about 1.3 g, hatchlings vary in weight between about 0.9 and 1.5 g depending on the size of egg from which they hatched. This is not surprising given the huge variation in egg weight (Chapter 7), but do such differences have consequences for the hatch rate or the growth rate, the fledging weight or survival of the chicks? In general, the hatching rate of Great Tit eggs in successful nests is high. Schifferli (1973) found that he could hatch 68 per cent of eggs if they were incubated artificially in an incubator, and the probability of an egg hatching was not related to its weight. Although Schifferli took only eggs that were due to hatch within a few days anyway, this rate was actually rather lower than what we usually observe in the nestboxes, where normally more than 90 per cent hatch (Perrins 1979). Perhaps this indicates (not surprisingly) that Great Tit females are more efficient at incubating their eggs than humans are.

More importantly, Schifferli returned those chicks that hatched to their nests and followed their growth through to fledging, relating their progress to the weights of the eggs from which they had hatched. He found that chicks from lighter eggs tended to grow more slowly during the first ten days than those from larger eggs, although in the majority of nests these slower-growing chicks were able to catch up by the time they fledged. The egg weight therefore had little effect on the likelihood that a chick would fledge. Furthermore, although (if all other things were equal) the maximum weight attained by a chick was related to its weight at hatching, this did

Figure 5 *Growth and development of Great Tit chicks. Figure 5a. shows the increase in weight, tarsus and wing lengths. Note that tarsus length and weight are fully developed by day 15 (hatch day is day 1) while wing length is only about two-thirds grown (full grown values are 70–78 mm). Major developmental events are also indicated. Figure 5b. shows the growth of the bill and gape. At day 15, bill depth is three-quarters and bill length is two-thirds of the final value. However, the gape width which is the principle target for the parents reaches a peak in size at about day 7 and then reduces due to the shrinkage of the gape flange.*

5(a)

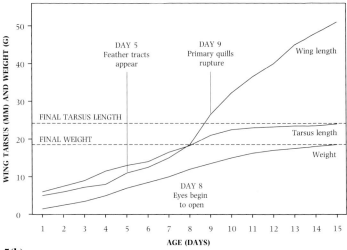

5(b)

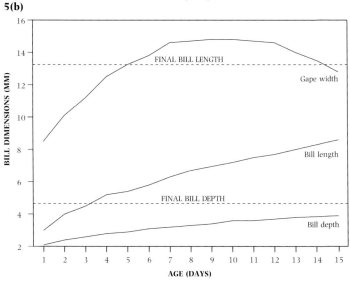

not affect its chances of survival after fledging. This is because, as we shall see, the number of competing chicks in the brood usually has a stronger influence on the final weight. In late nests, however, these slower-growing chicks were not able to make good their initial disadvantage, so that the egg weight did influence the chicks' chances of fledging. This means that for chicks in late nests, at a time when the caterpillar supply is declining, it may be advantageous to have hatched from a larger egg. This is particularly interesting, because females laying later in a season (whether their first or a subsequent clutch) tend to lay larger eggs (Chapter 7). Hence, while it is possible that the female is simply more able to produce larger eggs in the middle of the season because the food supply is better, it is also possible that the increased egg size is adaptive, as it gives the chicks a better start in life since, by the time their growth rate is at its greatest, the food supply will be in decline. Nevertheless, the benefit of increased egg size is not sufficient on its own to overcome the disadvantages that chicks suffer if they fledge late. Perrins (1970) summarized this situation clearly by suggesting that, overall, it is better to hatch early from a smaller egg than to hatch later from a larger one.

Feeding the chicks

For the first few days, the chicks cannot regulate their own body temperature and must be brooded by the female. This means that much of the food for the brood must be collected by the male during this time, the female gradually increasing her contribution from the second or third day so that by about day six she is providing as much as he is (Kluijver 1950). When provisioning the brood, the pair (and, for the reason just explained, especially the male) must take into account the chicks' size, because for the first week or so they will not be able to swallow large prey. For this reason, the size of prey brought is usually increased gradually until about day five, after which there is no further change (Royama 1970). In a classic study of nestling diet, Betts (1955) found that, in the first five days, prey items of 15 mm or more in length formed only 8 per cent of the chicks' diet and 65 per cent were less than 10 mm; between days six and ten, 58 per cent of items were 15 mm or more, and between then and fledging prey of this size formed 74 per cent of the diet, with caterpillars of up to 3 cm sometimes brought in. We know that this change in prey size reflects a decision by the parents rather than simply an increase in the size of prey available to them, because the same pattern occurs in nests started later in the season, when fewer small caterpillars are to be found (Royama 1970).

The change in adult diet from seed to caterpillars in the spring is associated with a considerable lengthening and, especially in males, also thinning (in depth) of the bill (Gosler 1987a). The horny covering (or rhamphotheca) of the bill is continually growing and being worn away by use. Although the increased length could result simply from a reduction in wear as the birds switch to a softer diet, this cannot, however, explain the reduction in depth. There is evidence that this narrowing is achieved actively by the birds increasing the frequency with which they wipe the bill on twigs in the spring compared with in the winter (Gosler 1987b). There is also some evidence that this active honing of the bill is undertaken because bill shape affects its efficiency in handling prey, and this may affect the quantity and quality of food that the brood receives (Gosler 1987c).

Apart from the change in prey size, only one systematic change in the chicks' diet has been detected (although not all studies have found this). Royama (1970) found that the proportion of the diet made up by spiders increased steadily after hatching, peaked at about day six or seven and then declined. He pointed out also that this occurred irrespective of habitat or time in the season, and that similar trends were detectable, though less clearly, in Betts's (1955) and Tinbergen's (1960) data from pine forest. Van Balen (1973) also found that spiders were fed especially to young chicks. Although the link is not proven, it is possible that this is related particularly to the development of feathers, since both feather keratin and spider proteins are rich in the sulphur-containing amino acid cystine. Also, feather development starts at around day five (opposite above) and, as shown by the curve of wing length in Figure 5a, feather growth rate is at its greatest between then and day nine when the quills rupture – at which point the feathers appear like tiny paintbrushes (opposite below).

Although the proportion of prey types other than caterpillars and spiders in the diet may not change systematically with the age of the brood, their representation is not necessarily constant from day to day or through the season. For example, prey other than caterpillars tends to feature more strongly in later nests (Van Balen 1973) and during cold or wet weather (Keil 1963). Dhondt (1971b) found that the survival rate of nestlings was very much lower in years when the temperature during the nestling period was lower, and this might be partly related to the poorer quality of food received by the brood under such conditions. The decline in food quality (and especially the reduction in the proportion of caterpillars in the diet) through the season in Oak woods accounts for the fact that chicks from later broods usually fledge at lower weights than those from earlier ones (Gosler 1987c).

There is much evidence that chick condition is related to food availability, but one example will serve to support this. Great Tit chicks in Wytham hatch into a situation of lengthening days, and in most years also rising daily temperatures and increasing insect abundance since most have fledged by the second week of June. The peak in caterpillar abundance, however, has usually passed by the time that chicks hatched in the last quarter of the season have fledged. In 1991, a sudden and prolonged cold spell with strong northerly winds from late April well into May provided an opportunity to look at chick development in a situation where weather conditions and food availability for later chicks were very much better, in Wytham, than for those hatched earlier. In an attempt to delay the hatch, in this year many females postponed incubation after the clutch had been completed (see Chapter 7). Nevertheless, this did not prevent the first broods from hatching in the first and second weeks of May. These early broods fared badly. Chicks in the first ten broods to hatch weighed only 16.5 g on average on day fifteen (by which time they should have reached their fledging weight). Overall, chicks fledging in the first half of the season weighed

ABOVE *Feather growth begins at five days. This is associated with a peak in the provision of spiders by the parents, probably necessary for good feather development.* BELOW *By ten days the feather quills have ruptured and the eyes have begun to open.*

Parental care in the Great Tit is comprehensive and includes nest-sanitation.
The chicks produce their faeces in neat, gelatinous sacs, which the parents remove
from the nest.

17.6 g. Chicks that fledged in the second half of the season, however, averaged 19.2 g in weight, and those in the last ten broods to fledge averaged 19.6 g, with many individuals achieving weights of more than 20 g.

As I described in Chapter 3, prey items tend to be delivered to the brood in 'runs' of a particular type. Not only does each parent tend to return with the same species of prey, but they both tend to return with the same type of prey before switching to another prey type (Royama 1970). Hence, when feeding the brood, the parents often appear to operate in a highly coordinated way. It is not entirely clear how they do this, because frequently they do not forage together, but rather they tend to alternate between being at the nest or out searching. It is possible that such coordination develops over time within a pair, and that experience of each other is necessary for it to work successfully. If true, then perhaps this partly explains the greater breeding success of pairs that have bred together previously (Perrins and McCleery 1985).

The rate at which Great Tit parents feed their brood is related to several factors other than the constraining one of food availability. Chief among these is the brood size. For example, I found in Wytham that, while a brood of six received 325 visits on their fourteenth day, a brood of eleven received 597. There are two important complications in this story which mean that these simple visit rates are not perfect indicators of the quantity of food actually received by a chick. The first is that, while visit rate increases with brood size, the rate of increase is often such that each chick in a large brood receives fewer feeds than each chick in a smaller brood. For example, Gibb and Betts (1963) found that chicks in a brood of seven each received 7.3 g of food per day, while those in a brood of nine received only 4.7 g each. The second complication is apparent from these figures, because they suggest that chicks in the larger brood were fed smaller prey; this is probably the case, for prey size is itself related to visit rate. Kluijver (1950) noted that, although late broods tended to receive fewer visits than earlier broods of the same size, the prey that they received were on average larger than those of the earlier broods. Van Balen (1973) also found that Great Tit parents, when feeding chicks more than eight days old visited more often if the average weight of each prey item was less. This might be explained by the optimal foraging theories described in Chapter 3. In particular, if parents forage further from the nest, they should spend longer searching for larger prey by way of compensation, and, because of the greater travelling time involved, we should also expect the birds to return to the nest less often when they are foraging further away. So, we should expect prey size and visit rate to be correlated also.

Because the amount of food received by each chick in a large brood tends to be less than that received by each in a smaller brood, the average weight of chicks fledging from large broods tends to be lower also. For this reason, the decision taken earlier by the female as to how many eggs to lay is often considered to reflect a trade-off between the quality (weight) and quantity of fledglings that will result (Smith *et al.* 1989). Whether it is better to produce many light fledglings rather than fewer heavier ones or not depends on conditions after fledging, and these differ between years in complex ways. We shall return to this important question in Chapter 11.

Since much of the early motivation for research on tits in nestboxes came from a desire to control insect pests, it is worth examining briefly at this point whether the tits do in fact have any effect on insect populations. Direct evidence from the study of insect populations suggests that, for a variety of reasons, insectivorous birds exert rather little control on the abundance of insects (Speight and Wainhouse 1989). In this respect, the effect of the birds on the abundance of their insect prey is similar to that of the tits' predators on tit numbers. There is, however, strong evidence from studies of the ecology of the birds themselves that, while they may not regulate insect populations, their effect is significant during the peak of caterpillar abundance. The evidence comes from the fact that different species compete for food at this time and that the presence of other tit species can influence the breeding success of Great Tits. Many bird species in oak woodland take advantage of the short-lived glut of caterpillars. For example, within a Great Tit territory, three other tit species, several warblers, Chaffinches, Blackbirds and even Great Spotted Woodpeckers may all be raising their broods on caterpillars. The Blue Tit in particular has been studied in this regard, and, while competition for nest holes usually results in a successful outcome for the Great Tits (simply because of their greater size), Blue Tits exact a more subtle revenge on their larger competitor (Minot and Perrins 1986). Ed Minot systematically removed Blue Tit chicks from nests in one part of Wytham and added them to nests in another area of the wood, thus reducing the overall Blue Tit requirement for food in the former area and increasing it in the latter, a third area was left unaltered as a control. He found that the average weight of Great Tit chicks at fledging was greater in the areas from which Blue Tits had been removed and lower where they had been added; the weights in the control areas were intermediate (Minot 1981). The reason why Blue Tits influence Great Tit breeding success rather than the reverse is that the smaller species takes smaller prey and tends to have its young in the nest a little earlier than the Great Tits; the Blue Tits therefore, on average, take younger caterpillars, so preventing them from growing into Great Tit food.

While the distribution and abundance of food must direct, and possibly constrain, the foraging behaviour of the pair, the relationship between brood size and visit rate indicates that the pair attempts to match its efforts to the needs of the brood. But how do the parents know this? Bengtsson and Rydén (1983) found that they could alter the visit rates of Great Tit parents by altering the volume of the chicks' begging calls inside the nestbox. They did this by playing recorded begging calls in the box. This simple experiment demonstrated that the parents gauged the hunger of the brood as a whole by how loudly they begged. They also found that the parents were not influenced by the condition of individual chicks or by which chick actually called loudest, since the largest chicks tended to be fed preferentially. It was the sound of the whole brood and not that of the hungriest chicks that was important to them.

Parental care and chick losses

Parental care in the Great Tit is comprehensive. Apart from the huge numbers of invertebrates that they bring to the brood, they also bring fine grit for the chicks' tiny gizzards and snail shell to provide additional calcium for their rapidly growing bones. On average, each chick may receive such a feed about once every one to two days (Royama 1970). Royama believed that snail shell was delivered to the chicks only as roughage rather than for the calcium content. In acid areas, however, where snails are scarce, problems related to the normal bone development of the chicks are encountered more frequently, suggesting a link between the two (J. Graveland pers. comm. and H. Crick pers. comm.).

As well as delivering the raw materials, the parents also remove the waste products. The chicks produce their faeces in neat gelatinous sacs, each weighing up to a gram. After feeding the brood, the parent waits for a chick to produce a faecal sac, removes it and takes it far from the nest. This is important, not only for nest sanitation, but because the nestlings' defecation rate rises from about twice a day per chick on day two to about ten times each day per chick on day fifteen (Royama 1966); if faecal sacs were simply dropped outside the nest, they would easily betray its position to predators.

Although their nest holes protect the tits well from predators, in fact allowing them to have a protracted nestling period compared with open nesters of similar size, a proportion of the broods is still lost to predators. The animals responsible for these losses vary between sites. In Wytham, Weasel and Great Spotted Woodpecker are the main predators of Great Tit broods in natural nest sites, but it is not always clear what has occurred when we find a failed nesting attempt. If the clutch or brood is still present, one assumes that the parents have deserted them, but we cannot know whether this was because they were disturbed at the nest, taken by a predator away from the nest (unless the parents are later found to be alive), or gave up for some other reason. Kluijver (1951) noted that 8.4 per cent of clutches were lost or deserted, while 17.9 per cent of broods were. This increase in the proportion of total losses after hatching has been found also at Wytham where, it seems that late broods are especially likely to suffer, and this is probably because the chicks are hungrier and therefore noisier, so they more easily give away their position (Dunn 1977). Since the noise from the nest and the parents' activity around it increase enormously after hatching, it is not surprising that they are more likely to suffer predation then. The likelihood that a pair will attempt to replace a lost clutch or brood declines as the season progresses.

In just two weeks, the chicks have increased fifteen-fold in weight. At fifteen days, their eyes are fully open and the chicks are alert and fully feathered.

Einloft-Achenbach and Schmidt (1984) found that Great Tit pairs in poorer habitats were much more likely to desert a breeding attempt than those in better habitat. For example, 28 per cent deserted in deciduous woodland, 40 per cent in coniferous woods and 61 per cent in the city of Frankfurt. It is not clear why this was so, but it was probably because the parents in poor habitats found insufficient food to meet both their own needs and those of the brood, so that they were forced through stress to give up.

This raises the question of how valuable the tits consider their brood to be. Since the chicks will not survive without their parents, it clearly makes

The Weasel is the principal predator of Great Tit eggs and chicks in Wytham.
Predation on the tits is more severe when the Weasel's preferred rodent prey is scarce.

no sense for them to put their own lives seriously at risk by trying to raise them, but how much of a risk are they prepared to take on their brood's behalf? Curio and his colleagues in Germany have studied this question by presenting a captive predator such as a Sparrowhawk or Pygmy Owl in a cage close to a Great Tit's nest and recording the parents' response. The birds reacted very much more strongly to a real predator than to a recording of its call (Curio 1979). Males responded more strongly than females and approached owls very much more closely than they would a Sparrowhawk, indicating that they were aware of the greater risk to themselves presented by the hawk (Curio *et al.* 1983). The intensity of defensive mobbing by the male was greater if he was defending an older brood, a larger brood, if it was later in the season, or if the density of neighbouring tits that might also come to help in mobbing was high. It was also greater if the female was present than if she was not (Regelmann and Curio 1983; Curio 1987). This last point is curious, for the evidence suggests that the female's presence stimulated the male to mob more persistently.

Taking all of these observations together, it seems that the intensity with which a Great Tit defends its brood reflects the value of the brood in terms of its contribution to the tit's lifetime reproductive success. Older chicks are more likely to fledge than younger chicks because most of the hazards of the nestling stage have passed, so the brood is more valuable later. Later in the season, there is less time or food available to start a replacement clutch, so that the present brood must be more valuable. Because such behaviour is obviously adaptive, we can assume that it has been optimized by thousands of years of natural selection. Nevertheless, that these small birds weigh up so many factors (whether consciously or not) when deciding whether and how to mob a predator surely serves to instil wonder in the observer.

9

THE FIRST
THREE MONTHS

GREAT Tit broods fledge after 19–21 days in the nest. The decision to fledge is made, at least in part, by the parents. During the last few days they reduce the amount of food that they deliver to the chicks, so that the brood is forced to fledge largely by hunger. Indeed, as we shall see, the parents will manipulate the course of their offspring's development to independence from here on by altering the proportion of the brood's food that is received from them. For a few days before fledging, the chicks are more active inside the nest chamber.They jump around in the nest while exercising their wings to help strengthen the muscles in preparation for their first flight. Where previously all food had been delivered into the nest, now, some feeds are simply made at its entrance, with chicks clambering up to receive the parent's offering. This also means that towards the end of the nestling period fewer of the chicks' faecal sacs are removed, so the nest will often become increasingly soiled. Finally, whereas the female always roosts at night with the brood during the nestlings' first week (and most do so during the second also), during the last days many females increasingly roost away from the nest, as indeed their partners had done throughout the breeding cycle. Hence, there is a gradual reduction in contact between parents and brood towards the latter stages of nestling development.

Fledging usually occurs in the morning, which gives the family time to familiarize themselves a little with their surroundings while it is still light (Perrins 1979; Lemel 1989b). During fledging, the parents may entice the chicks to jump by flying to the nest entrance with food and then carrying it away again, as if telling them to 'come and get it'. Lemel (1989b) studied how the order in which the chicks left the nest was influenced by their body condition. A chick's condition was described as its weight relative to size, so a bird that was heavy for its size was said to be in good condition and vice versa. He found that the second chick to leave was generally the heaviest relative to its size (i.e., in the best condition), and that the rest of the brood generally left in order of decreasing body condition; the last to leave would be the chick with the poorest condition. The first chick to leave, however, was one in intermediate condition. Why is this so? Before fledging, nestling Great Tits develop a dominance hierarchy based strictly on size. This is a matter of physical strength: the heaviest is the most dominant, and the least dominant is the lightest (Garnett 1981). Such dominance comes into play when, for example, the nestlings compete for food, so that larger chicks will often tend to be in better condition also. Lemel found that, once one chick had fledged, the parents concentrated their attention on that fledgling. Hence, once fledging had begun, the best place for a chick switched rapidly from the nest to the outside, and the scramble to fledge then reflected the order of dominance in the brood. Before any chick has fledged, however, the outside is the best place only for hungrier chicks, because of the many new risks that must be faced outside the box. The first to succumb to the parents' enticements, therefore, is generally not the most dominant, but the most dominant of the hungrier nestlings. Social dominance features in the Great Tit's world even at this early stage.

Around the time of fledging, the parents respond with a characteristic display to the sound of a chick alarm call near the nest. They glide over the site of the calling chick, while giving their own hissing call. At the end of the flight, which is often at low level, the bird alights and displays its belly-stripe to the ground while making (what appears to be) an exaggerated searching movement from side to side (see overleaf); in this, the body is held horizontally with the wings held away from it and the neck extended. This continues for some seconds before another pass is made, and so on. Although it appears that the bird is searching for the source of the sound, it sometimes displays in this way away from the calling chick, suggesting a ritualized display. This is particularly interesting because the response develops gradually as the chicks mature. For example, while most parents do not respond in this way to a recorded chick call on the brood's tenth day, most do so on the eighteenth. Perrins (1979) suggests that a similar and equivalent display in the Blue Tit probably serves to distract predators from the calling chick. Certainly the effect is striking.

The begging calls of the fledglings are the same as those used by older nestlings when hungry and sound something like a loud, slightly nasal and rapidly repeated 'Do-Do-Dee-Dee-Dee-Do-Do', etc. (unlike the high-pitched squeaking of younger nestlings). These are accompanied by the rapid wing-shivering display used by most passerine fledglings when soliciting food, and by the female when food-begging from the male earlier in the spring. From about mid May, many woods ring with these persistent begging calls. Broods stay with their parents (especially the male) for a variable period after fledging. This is the 'dependent period', and Riddington (1992) found that its average length in Wytham was nineteen days, although it varied from thirteen to 25 days. The female may start a second clutch now, but this will depend on the size of the first brood, the time in the season and the population density (see also Chapter 2; and Kluijver 1951; Slagsvold 1984; Tinbergen 1987; Smith et al. 1987; Lindén 1988). The rate at which the fledglings learn to fend for themselves depends on the willingness of their parents to feed them. Davies (1978) found that the proportion of food hand-raised fledglings obtained by their own efforts was directly related to the length of time that he made them beg for food before feeding them: if they were forced to beg for longer, they would more rapidly learn to manipulate objects around them and to find their own food than if they were fed instantly. He described this simply in terms of the profitability (food gain over time) of the two sources of food, namely parent versus self-feeding. If the relative profitability of begging dropped below that of self-feeding, then the fledgling would be forced to develop its own foraging skills more quickly.

I know of no evidence that Great Tit parents can actually recognize their own young (either by sight or by sound) once they have left the nest, although there is much to suggest that they cannot. First, as shown above, parents respond to a recording of any Great Tit chick call with a distraction display which might involve some risk to themselves. Since parents even take into consideration the value of their own brood when assessing whether to mob predators (Chapter 8), it seems very unlikely that they would act in this way for a chick that was not their own if they could identify it as such. Perhaps the best evidence, however, is that during the dependent period different family parties sometimes come into contact. It is

When the time comes, the parents encourage the chicks to leave the nest by appearing briefly at the entrance with food, before flying away again.

not unusual, in the resulting confusion, for fledglings to become separated from their own family group and to tag along with the other family. This seems not to matter a great deal, as the unwitting foster parents feed their newly acquired adoptees along with their own brood. Indeed, it is not unknown for dependent 'broods' to consist entirely of adopted chicks, none of which is related to the adults caring for them (R. Riddington pers. comm.). We have already seen from the various brood-manipulation experiments, in which chicks were switched between nests, that parents readily accept into the nest chicks that are not their own. Furthermore, there are many cases where a Blue Tit nest that already contains eggs has been taken over by Great Tits. Remarkably, these eggs are often incubated along with the Great Tit's own, whereupon some hatch and a few even fledge. We do not know what becomes of these Blue Tits.

Where do parents take their dependent broods? Drent (1984) believed that they led them to the area in which the male had spent his own formative weeks. It is still not entirely clear whether this is true, but recent work by Simon Verhulst and Roelof Hut on Vlieland suggests that it may indeed be (pers. comm.). One reason why this may happen is that it may be the only area that the male knows where there had been sufficient food

Around fledging time, the birds perform a ritualized searching and mobbing display in response to a chick alarm call near the nest. In the search display, the body is rotated horizontally from side to side, while the wings are held away from the body.

at that particular time in earlier years – after all, he survived as a result of being taken there. It could be that the male's feeding area is used in preference to the female's, because males usually settle closer to their birth site than females, so that his area is simply closer than hers. Although this is all highly speculative at present, it could, if correct, have far-reaching implications for the patterns of dispersal and survival that we see.

Independence and dispersal of young

The dependent period is a dangerous time for the young birds, as they have to learn several essential survival skills simultaneously, such as flight, feeding and predator avoidance. Although Sparrowhawks take most young Great Tits within a few days of fledging, the heaviest losses, however, appear to occur when the family bands break up and the juveniles must be fully independent (Riddington 1992). Gibb (1954a) documented the average increase in feeding skills of the Marley Wood Great Tit population as a whole, by recording the percentage of observations of juveniles in which the birds fed themselves. During the third week of June 1950, he found that 15 per cent of juveniles were feeding themselves but none was seen feeding intensely for itself. One month later this had risen to 63 per cent, and in half the observations the juveniles concerned were feeding intensely (indicating a high degree of coordination). In July and August, they may spend more than 70 per cent of their time foraging, and over the next few months they increase the diversity of their foraging sites also. For many populations, this is the period when the greatest losses are incurred and when the greatest degree of population-mixing and juvenile dispersal occurs. It is also the period in the bird's year about which we know least.

For the Great Tit, dispersal and settlement are inextricably linked to social dominance, so it is not surprising to find that those factors that influence dominance, such as size and fledging date, also have a bearing on dispersal. We have seen that larger young are dominant even when still in the nest, and it will be recalled from Chapter 1 that males are on average some 4 per cent larger than females. This means that, if food is short, the resulting competition between nestlings tends to favour males. Dhondt (1970a) found that when the Great Tit population density was high (more competition for the available food) proportionately more males fledged than females. While this could be explained by the bias in nestling mortality just described, he also suggested that it resulted because more males than females actually hatched in such years (Dhondt 1970b). This could happen only if the mother altered the sex ratio of the eggs that she laid under different conditions of population density, and this remains a subject of debate (Slagsvold and Amundsen 1992).

We have seen that sex is a major determinant of social dominance in the Great Tit. Perrins (1965) found that in most years heavier chicks were more likely than lighter ones to survive the first three months, but this is related also to the fact that earlier-fledged young are very much more likely to survive than late young, and earlier young tend to be heavier than later young. There is now considerable evidence that the poorer survival of later-fledged young is due to their need to compete for food and space with older, more experienced youngsters from earlier broods (Kluijver 1971; Slagsvold 1984; Sandell and Smith 1991; Verhulst 1992; Riddington 1992). Since the larger males are able to settle closer to their birth place, it is not surprising that females tend to disperse further than males before their first breeding attempt (Kluijver 1951; Dhondt 1979; Greenwood et al. 1979b). Because of their lower status, later young also tend to disperse further than earlier young, although this effect is found in smaller, more fragmented populations such as those studied in Belgium, rather than in large tracts of woodland like Wytham (Dhondt and Hublé 1968b; Greenwood et al 1979b). Indeed, in fragmented habitat, Dhondt & Hublé found that, although late young were twice as likely to leave the woods in which they hatched, the overall survival rate (actually the rate of retrapping, rather than survival) to the following year was the same for both groups of juveniles at about 5 per cent. It is perhaps surprising that, although there is so much evidence that competition drives dispersal and mortality in these populations, there is little to indicate that dispersal is related to the population's density.

For most juveniles, high summer is spent in flocks, roaming the countryside with others of their own and other species. Few of them will survive to the autumn. There are many reasons for this, some of which have already been discussed, but an additional stress for the young birds is that, on top of everything else, they must undergo a partial moult at this time. In the next chapter we shall look at the details of Great Tit moult, both for juveniles and for adults, and consider how successive moults change the plumage with the bird's advancing age.

10

MOULT

MOULT is the periodic replacement of the plumage. This is necessary because feathers become worn with time, so gradually losing their insulating properties and affecting the aerodynamic efficiency of structures such as the wings and tail. This wear results from direct abrasion caused by the bird's surroundings, from the action of sunlight, and from the insatiable attentions of parasites such as feather lice (Mallophaga). Feathers are composed largely of the protein keratin (like our own hair and nails), and the plumage of a small bird such as a Bullfinch may make up 10 per cent of its live weight or 40 per cent of its total dry weight (Newton 1966). Hence, the replacement of that plumage is expensive in terms of the demands that it makes for both protein and energy (Murphy and King 1991). Measurements of other passerines of comparable weight suggest that, during moult, a Great Tit may need to increase its intake of protein to about 10 per cent of its daily food intake, and its daily energy intake to about 20 kcal (Dolnik and Gavrilov 1979; Murphy and King 1991). Compared with the figures given in Chapter 3, these represent increases of about 25 per cent and 11 per cent respectively.

Given its costs, it is not surprising that birds time the moult so that it overlaps as little as possible with other expensive activities such as breeding or migration. The extent to which they need to reduce that overlap, however, depends on the availability of food and the time available for the moult's completion in relation to those other activities. This means that species that breed in the Arctic are more constrained with regard to moult than those in the tropics (Ginn and Melville 1983). Such general patterns of adaptation as we can see in comparisons of different species suggest that those with a wide geographical distribution (especially of latitude), such as the Great Tit, may be particularly interesting, since there must be great differences between populations in the balance of the costs and benefits of moulting at different times. As with so many aspects of the biology of this bird, however, a description of moult must be introduced with the caveat that most of what we know comes from studies of northern populations, and especially from Belgium, Britain and Finland. Nevertheless, the extent of moult in southern Europe seems to be similar.

The Great Tit is typical of most northern passerines, and of all *Parus* species, in having one moult each year. This occurs at about the same time in summer in both adults and juveniles, but its extent and therefore also its duration differ between these age classes. It is this difference in the extent of moult that allows us to distinguish birds in their first year of life. In adults, moult begins with the dropping of the innermost primary flight feather around the middle of June, although, exceptionally, this can occur as early as the end of May. As with other passerines, the ten primaries are dropped sequentially together with their coverts, each one being pushed out by the newly growing feather when the previous one in the sequence is about one third to a half grown. This system means that while the bird's flight may suffer some little impairment, it is never flightless. In the Great Tit, full primary replacement takes about seventy to one hundred days but there are differences between populations. In Belgium it may take 68 to ninety days in females and 85 to one hundred days in males (Dhondt 1973), while at Oulu (65 °N) in Finland it may be completed in seventy to 75 days in both sexes (Orell and Ojanen (1980). In the whole population, the period over which moulting adults can be found would be about one hundred to 120 days, so ending in September. Since most of the moult of other feather tracts occurs during the period of this primary moult, differences in moult between sexes and populations can be described in terms of the primary moult.

Males are generally the first in the population to commence moult. In Wytham, most adult males are starting primary moult at the beginning of June, often while they still have dependent young in the nest. Females start a week to ten days later. In Finland, the first males in moult are encountered in the last week of June and the first females in the second week of July. Populations also differ in the overlap between moult and the production of a second brood. In Wytham, those few adults that attempt a second brood have usually started primary replacement by the time the chicks are one week old. At Oulu, where second broods are very much more frequent, Orell and Ojanen (1980) found much the same pattern, with 6.8 per cent of males in moult while the first brood was in the nest but 87.5 per cent in moult when feeding a second brood. No female was found in moult while tending a first brood, but 94.4 per cent were moulting by the time the second brood fledged. In Belgium, Dhondt (1973) found that birds with second broods started moult some three weeks later than those not making a subsequent nesting attempt. Orell and Ojanen (1983b) suggest that the timing of moult may be so critical for Great Tits in northern populations that it may have been responsible for the very sharp decline in clutch size that occurs with date there: in other words, females are trying to reduce the duration of the breeding season as much as possible to lessen the conflict for resources between breeding and moult. It would clearly be interesting to know how the birds tackle these problems in southern Europe.

Moult of the six secondary flight feathers starts with the outermost at about the time the third to fifth primaries are dropped, and proceeds sequentially in the same way as primary moult, but towards, rather than away from, the body. At the same time, the three tertials (sometimes referred to as the innermost secondaries) moult, and the twelve tail feathers begin to moult sequentially from the central pair outwards (centrifugally). Body moult also commences at this time, so that a great wave of moult activity starts suddenly halfway through primary replacement. This is associated with (and probably causes) a slowing in the rate at which the remaining primaries are replaced, although there is no change in the growth rates of the individual feathers (Dhondt 1973). The tail and tertial moult is usually completed before the end of primary moult, but secondary and body moult may continue for some days afterwards.

The post-juvenile moult, which replaces the plumage grown in the nest, involves fewer feather tracts than that of the adult moult, although its extent varies much more between individuals. The main difference from the adult is that, as in most northern passerines, the primaries and their coverts, and the secondaries, are never moulted. The body feathers are all replaced to give the adult-type plumage. Occasionally, a few yellow cheek feathers may be retained. Now it gets interesting, because the extent to which the tail feathers, tertials, greater (secondary) coverts and alula moult varies between populations and sexes and also with the date of fledging, and is undoubtedly related to the availability of food for the moulting juvenile (Gosler 1991). In Belgium, this moult starts about 75 days after fledging for first-brood young, or about 65 days in second-brood young. Here, also, most juveniles replace the tail completely, while in Britain tail moult varies between populations from a few central feathers being replaced to 80 per cent of birds replacing them all (Ginn and Melville 1983). In Belgium, 41 per cent moult the alula while a further 6 per cent moult it on one wing only. In a Hertfordshire population, only 8 per cent moulted the whole alula (Flegg and Cox 1969). In all these studies, males are more likely than females to have a complete moult of any given tract. Although it starts later than the adult moult, the full juvenile moult ends at about the same time, in mid to late September.

Perhaps the most variable component of the juvenile moult is that of the greater coverts. In Wytham, the proportion of females with incomplete greater-covert moult (i.e., where one or more outer juvenile coverts is retained) varies between years from 5 per cent to more than 40 per cent, while it is rare for more than 20 per cent of males to arrest moult in this way. In Belgium, only 5 per cent of females failed to complete greater-covert moult, and again this was even rarer in males. In both these populations, later-fledged young were less likely to complete this moult (Dhondt 1973; Gosler 1991). In Killarney, south-west Ireland, Terry Carruthers and I have recently found incomplete moult of greater coverts to be the case more often than not; and, whereas in Wytham it would be very rare to find birds with more than two unmoulted coverts, in Killarney this is common and we have seen two females in which no greater coverts had been moulted at all. Again, more males than females completed this moult. It is tempting to consider the moult of this tract as an indicator (a kind of bioassay) of food availability for the bird during moult. It is also tempting to ask whether other Great Tits can use this sign as an indicator of an individual's condition, because the extent of greater-covert moult is indeed correlated with other measures of body condition after that moult (Gosler 1991).

The difference in extent between post-juvenile and post-nuptial moults means that first-year birds can still be distinguished from adults after moult. Because the extent of moult of the tail, greater coverts and alula is so variable in first-years, these are poor criteria upon which to base a diagnosis of age. That is, while a bird with juvenile outer greater coverts must be a first-year, those which have moulted the whole tract are not necessarily adults. However, since the juvenile primary coverts are never replaced in the post-juvenile moult, these present the best criterion for ageing. The juvenile primary coverts are more pointed than the adult's and show a slight greenish hue. This is generally more pronounced in females, and some males can be difficult to age. There is a simple solution to this, which I have found to be infallible after checking the ages of many thousands of Great Tits whose exact age was known because they had been ringed as nestlings. The lesser and median (secondary) coverts are always moulted in birds of all ages and replaced by blue feathers: in the adult, the blue of the primary coverts is identical to that of these lessers and medians; in first-years, however, there is always some difference in colour between these tracts, so, if the primary and lesser coverts are not absolutely identical in shade of blue, the bird is a first-year. The variation in the intensity of blue in the primary coverts of first-year males is interesting in itself, since it seems that they are trying to emulate older birds with whom they may later have to compete for a mate. There is still a great deal that we do not know about the causes of the subtle differences in colour of different tracts.

ABOVE *The 'upper flash' of the Great Tit as seen from above and behind as the bird breaks cover. The flash of contrasting wing bars and tail edgings may briefly confuse a predator.* LEFT *The contrasting face pattern of the Great Tit always indicates where the bird is facing even at some distance. This pattern might have earned the bird its old English name of Ox-eye.*

*Wing detail of a first-winter male Great Tit. The primary coverts are blue-green, contrasting with the blue of the moulted lesser coverts to the upper left. Compare this with the adult male (*BOTTOM*)*

*Wing detail of a first-winter female Great Tit. The contrast between the green primary and blue lesser coverts is clearer than in the first-winter male (*TOP*). Note also the unmoulted (outermost) greater covert (left).*

Wing detail of adult male Great Tit showing rounded, blue primary coverts (centre right) and no contrast between these and the other covert tracts.

The possible significance of plumage pattern

It is clear that many aspects of the moult and of colour variation in the Great Tit are adaptive, probably in ways that we can only wonder about at present. In the rest of this chapter, I shall break away from the factual presentation that has characterized the rest of the book and indulge a little in some pure speculation. Why has the plumage of the Great Tit evolved in the way that it has? Which of its many distinctive features might be adaptive and which might have been carried along with the evolution of other traits through being linked genetically with them? In some respects, the Great Tit's plumage is like a military battledress. The underlying colours of green and yellow are cryptic and provide some degree of countershading (lighter below, darker above). A Great Tit foraging in the tree canopy for caterpillars in summer can be very difficult to distinguish from the leaves in which it is searching, since the tit resembles the leaves in both size and colour. The striped pattern of the upperparts produced by wingbars and contrasting outer tail feathers produces a flash – the upper flash – when the bird flies from cover, which may just be sufficient distraction or confusion to a hawk to save its life. Superimposed on this camouflage are the bird's badges of status and rank – the belly-stripe, variously coloured primary and greater coverts etc, and the glossiness of the head. The head pattern itself is particularly notable. The symmetrical white cheeks contrasting with the black cap, chin and throat act in such a way that an observer can always tell where the bird is looking. This is true even at a considerable distance, when the dark eyes are not visible. This is probably how it acquired its old country name of 'Ox-eye' in Britain. In so sociable a bird, could this be an advantage? Finally, there is the eye colour itself. Jon King and John Muddeman (pers. comm.) have recently noticed that the eye colour of young Great Tits is rather greyer than the rich reddish-brown of the adults. A similar difference exists in many passerines. Does this colour change also serve some purpose?

11

SURVIVAL AND RECRUITMENT

IN this book, I have described numerous examples of adaptation in the
Great Tit, i.e., characteristics of the form, physiology or behaviour of the
bird that have a bearing upon the fitness of individuals. The spacing of
breeding pairs and formation of winter flocks, the pattern of the plumage,
the nature of the song, of the diet and of foraging behaviour, the timing of
breeding and moult, the shape of the bill and the number of eggs in a
clutch are all examples of such adaptation. Adaptation is the inevitable
outcome of the fact that individuals in a population differ genetically and
not all are equally likely to survive to breed. In other words, there is
natural selection. We have already seen that certain characteristics of
juvenile Great Tits such as the date on which they fledge and their weight
at fledging predispose them differently to survive the many hazards that
await them. Hence, a key element in the evolution over time of adaptation
is the pattern of survival and, crucially, of recruitment to the breeding
population. In this chapter, we shall consider the causes of mortality at
different times of the year and try to relate these to the changes that occur
from year to year in the density of breeding pairs in Great Tit populations.

First, it is worth reiterating some basic arithmetic. It will be recalled
that, on average, about half of the breeding adults die each year. This
means that, in the case of a stable population (which is usually the case in
our study populations), an average of only one chick is being recruited
from each breeding pair in each year. Put another way, averaged across
the whole population, each adult is simply replacing itself before it dies.
Since an average of five chicks is fledged per pair (including pairs that fail
completely), this means that four of these, or 80 per cent of the young
produced each year, either die or emigrate. These losses are not evenly
distributed with respect to the parent population, since most recruits are
produced by a small proportion of the breeding pairs (Chapter 4). In the
Hoge Veluwe in the Netherlands, for example, 50 per cent of females
recruit no young, 24 per cent produce one recruit, 9 per cent produce two
and fewer than 5 per cent of females have more than five young recruited
(Van Noordwijk and Van Balen 1988). The pattern for Wytham is similar,
although here 64 per cent of females have no young recruited. Although
the average adult survival rate each year is 50 per cent in Wytham, it has
varied between 29 per cent and 73 per cent over the years. Estimates of
the average juvenile survival rate have varied between years from 3 per cent
to 21 per cent, although these figures are not strictly comparable with
those for the adults because they are influenced more by losses due to

emigration. Nevertheless, we can say that juvenile survival rates appear to be more variable than those of the adults, since they have varied by some sevenfold compared with the twofold to threefold variation of the adults (McCleery and Perrins 1989). This means that juvenile survival rate has a much greater impact on the change in overall population size from year to year than does adult survival rate. This has been known for many years (Perrins 1966), and may be summarized by saying that changes in population size from year to year are caused largely by changes in the fortunes of the young of the previous year.

From the figures given above, it seems that some individuals are more likely to recruit young than others. It is important to realize that, although the parents may be only replacing themselves and maintaining a stable population, this is not the 'aim' of the individual. Each breeding Great Tit in the population actually 'wants' to have as many of its own young recruited as possible. The fact that we are not knee-deep in Great Tits merely indicates that there are severe constraints on the birds' ability to achieve this. Some of the factors that determine an individual's chances of survival, such as the fledging date, and weight, are, up to a point, within the parents' control, while others, such as the food supply, population density and intensity of predation, are not. If the parents can gauge what the strengths of these environmental influences will be later in the year when their young have fledged, they may, however, be able to tailor their chicks (in terms of quality versus quantity of young (*see* Chapter 8) so as to give them the best possible chance of surviving. Although there are obviously limits to the female's ability to make such predictions, there is, nevertheless, evidence that she attempts to. Because competition for resources between the young tits is fierce after fledging, when the population density is high, it is better to produce a few, high-quality chicks, which will be better able to compete and obtain a territory, than to produce many chicks of poorer quality, which will almost certainly die (Perrins 1988). The fact that females usually reduce the size of the clutch that they lay when the population density is high, despite being able to lay more eggs, strongly suggests that they are making such a trade-off. It is important to realize, however, that this reduction in clutch size is not nearly sufficient to compensate for the increase in population density so that the density, of fledglings will still be greater in a year of high breeding density.

Causes of death of young

Ultimately, there are just two significant causes of death for the young birds. These are starvation and predation. For the nestlings, starvation obviously results when the parents are unable to provide sufficient suitable food (caterpillars), but there can be several reasons for this. The density of caterpillars may be low, or they may be harder to find because of poor weather, or the pair may have misjudged the peak in caterpillar abundance. Parents will often compensate for this by bringing other sorts of prey such as flies, hoverflies and even beetles (as often happens in late nests in oak woodland), but such indigestible items reduce the chicks' growth rate and may

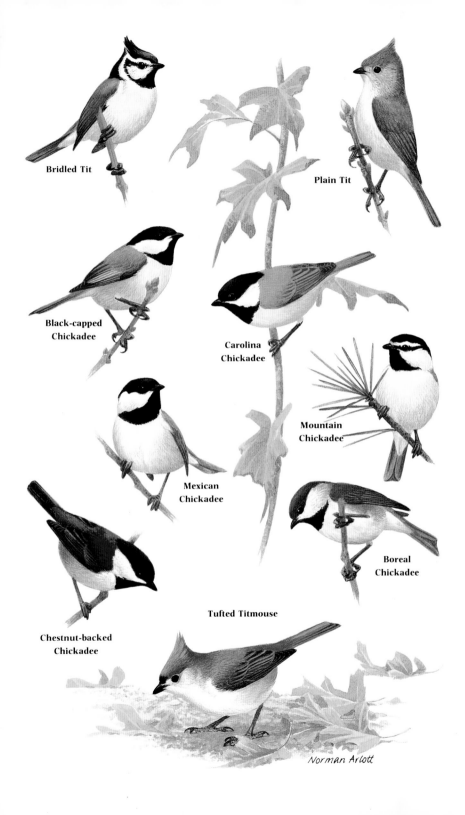

Bridled Tit

Plain Tit

**Black-capped
Chickadee**

**Carolina
Chickadee**

**Mountain
Chickadee**

**Mexican
Chickadee**

**Boreal
Chickadee**

Tufted Titmouse

**Chestnut-backed
Chickadee**

Norman Arlott

themselves contribute to a higher mortality in these broods. Certainly such chicks sometimes show indications of gastric disorders, their plumage becoming soiled by their own faeces, and this may cause them to chill. There is a further reason, related to diet, why late broods fare less well than early young. This is that, although there may be no shortage in the numbers of caterpillars available in the woods, there is a change in the digestibility of the larvae themselves. I mentioned in Chapter 2 that the leaves of broadleaved trees such as oak accumulate tannins and other chemicals as the season progresses, in an effort to reduce their digestibility to the insects. These chemicals subsequently accumulate in the guts of the caterpillars feeding on them. Perrins (1976) found that hand-raised nestling Blue Tits grew at a slower rate if fed a diet of caterpillars containing a higher concentration of tannin, and it is likely that the same would be true for Great Tits. This also explains why parents sometimes remove the heads of caterpillars, so allowing them to draw out and discard the gut before feeding the prey to the brood. There is yet a further risk to late broods which is related to the poorer quality of diet. Hungry chicks are noisy chicks, and noisy chicks are more likely to betray their presence to predators. This simple relationship probably explains the higher rate of brood losses often observed among later nests and larger broods (Dunn 1977; Perrins 1979). There can be no doubt that some predators use the sound of a hungry brood to locate them. For example, the characteristic sign that a brood has been taken from its nestbox by a Great Spotted Woodpecker is a hole drilled in the side of the box at the level of the calling chicks. In contrast, a Grey Squirrel enlarges the entrance hole by gnawing around the edge until it is large enough for it to enter the box (page 105).

In addition to the problems faced directly by chicks under poor conditions, parents that are stressed also seem more likely to desert their brood. This is suggested by the higher desertion rates observed in poorer-quality habitats described in Chapter 8. The desertion risk also seems to be greater during very wet or cold seasons, or if one of the parents is taken by a predator. Although the remaining parent will often battle on alone, this will usually result in the brood fledging at a very low weight. There is little to indicate that population density itself has a direct influence on the food availability for the pair, but, we should not necessarily expect to see such an influence if the female has already compensated adequately for a high density by reducing her brood size, and so this does not mean that there is no influence. Furthermore, since most food for the brood is collected within a few tens of metres of the nest, and each pair has more or less exclusive access to this area (at least with regard to other Great Tits), we may expect the density of breeding pairs to influence a pair's success only when food is already scarce for other reasons. This is because, under such circumstances, the parents

---

The nine tit species of North America. The Tufted Titmouse is the largest of these and shows a number of ecological parallels with the European Great Tit although its social organization is quite different. The chief similarities between the two species are in their foraging habits since beechmast, which is found on the ground, is a principal winter food for both.

would have to search for food further from their own nest, and this is more likely to bring them into conflict with neighbours if they are nearby.

A link between fledgling weight and likelihood of survival has been known for many years (Perrins 1963); but why are heavy chicks more likely to survive? A chick's weight has two components: the bird's size and its condition. Put simply, a heavy chick may be heavy because it is large, or because it carries more fat (or both). If heavy chicks are more likely to survive because they carry more fat, it suggests that they may simply be better able to survive for longer when food is scarce shortly after independence. If heavy chicks survive better because they are larger, however, it must almost certainly be because of their greater ability when competing directly with other Great Tits. Garnett (1976) found that, in fact, most of the variation in fledging weight of Great Tits was due to variation in size rather than fat reserves, so that a story involving social dominance is most likely. Furthermore, by looking directly at the body condition of chicks near to fledging, rather than simply their weight, Lindén (1990) found that very fat chicks were actually marginally less likely to be recruited than their slightly leaner siblings, although it is not really clear why this should be.

The greatest losses in the population occur in this cohort of juveniles during the three or four months after fledging. Dhondt (1979) estimated that in southern Sweden only 22 per cent of chicks were still alive at the start of September, although the losses were relatively greater in years when the density was higher, i.e. mortality was density-dependent. He further estimated that the juvenile mortality rate was constant through the summer at about 13 per cent per week. Riddington (1992) found a similar pattern in Wytham, although there was a peak in mortality around the time of independence. Density-dependent losses have now been reported in most populations studied. O'Connor (1980) analysed the Great Tit population data held by the British Trust for Ornithology (BTO). These data are particularly interesting because they were collected at many sites across the country, rather than at a single location, and therefore give an impression of the mechanics of a national population. He found that, while density-dependent influences were strong in woodland sites, they were weaker in farmland plots, suggesting that the latter acted as secondary or buffer areas that filled up only when the woodland habitats were occupied; nationally, an increase in the density of the Great Tit population was associated with a reduction in the average clutch size and fledging success, while the average dispersal distance and mortality rate of fledged juveniles were increased.

It is a curious feature of these summer losses that the number of young dying appears to be related partly to the abundance of beechmast during the following winter, even though the mast will not be available to them until October and even then few tits will feed on it for another month. This problem was recognized many years ago, and it should be said that even now the processes involved are not entirely clear, so the story that I shall outline is still somewhat speculative. It is important to understand that the beechmast crop that becomes available in October is the result of nearly two years of flower and fruit development by the trees, and is therefore strongly influenced by the summer temperatures of the year before the one in which the crop falls: i.e., the October 1921 Beech crop was influenced by the summer temperatures of 1920 (Matthews 1955). Related to this, and probably also as a strategy to foil their seed predators, individual Beech trees never produce a good crop in two successive years. Since fruiting tends to be remarkably synchronous among trees over large areas, this means that good and bad crops tend to alternate through the years (Lebreton 1990). Now the Beech crop does have a real effect on survival of both juveniles and adults once they have come to feed on it (Van Balen 1980; Clobert *et al.* 1988). So the relationship between a good Beech crop next winter and the juvenile survival the previous summer results not from its own direct actions, but from the fact that those young birds had hatched during a year of comparatively low population density, caused by a poor Beech crop the previous winter. If the population density is low when the young birds fledge, we can expect proportionately more to survive to the autumn. If they do, their chances of surviving the winter are then similar to those of the adults (Hildén 1978; Schmidt and Wolff 1985).

Because of their wanderings in search of territory, the juveniles are the most mobile section of the Great Tit population. It is therefore often difficult to distinguish deaths in the population from losses due to emigration, which may themselves be density-dependent (O'Connor 1980). To accommodate this problem, we have to make the assumption that the survival rate of emigrants is the same as for those that remain and are recruited, although we know that this is unlikely because of the overwhelming evidence that juvenile survival is related to social dominance

Predators leave different signs of their identity at the nest. While Grey Squirrels enlarge the entrance by gnawing, Great Spotted Woodpeckers drill into the nest at chick level.

(de Laet 1985b). Hence, we should always expect the emigrant population to include the least dominant birds, and for this reason we might expect their subsequent survival rate to be poor. It is also commonly assumed in bird population studies that immigration and emigration are reciprocal processes, and that we can ascertain something about the birds that leave the population from a study of the immigrants that are subsequently caught breeding in the wood. However, this is probably not correct, either. Dhondt and Hublé (1968b) showed that later-fledged young were more likely to emigrate than earlier young. This is, of course, entirely consistent with the argument that emigration is driven partly by dominance, since we know that earlier young tend to be dominant (Chapter 9). Later-fledged young, however, are also less likely to complete post-juvenile moult and so are more likely than early young to retain juvenile greater coverts after moult (Chapter 10). Hence, if immigrants and emigrants are equivalent groups of birds, we should expect more immigrants than residents to retain juvenile coverts. This, however, is not the case (Gosler 1991).

Survival

Because of the comparative mobility of juveniles, rather more attention has been paid in recent years to the survival of established adults (Clobert *et al.* 1988). In this group, we are more likely to be able to attribute losses between breeding seasons to mortality rather than to emigration. Work on the adult population strongly confirms the influence of social dominance in determining survival: males are consistently more likely to survive than females (Orell and Ojanen 1979; Clobert *et al.* 1988), and resident males are more likely to survive than immigrants (Clobert *et al.* 1988). Curiously, immigrant females at Wytham have a higher survival rate than resident females and, although there is some evidence that they may be socially dominant to the residents, it is not clear why (Clobert *et al.* 1988). These differences in quality between immigrant and resident adults is also reflected in the number of their young that are subsequently recruited. McCleery and Clobert (1990) found that resident males consistently recruited more young than immigrant males. Resident females, however, also recruited more young than did immigrants, although the strength of this relationship varied from year to year. It is not clear whether these differences reflect differences in survival or emigration, and these areas are still under investigation.

Since females are less likely to survive, and they disperse further than males, we might expect there to be a small set of males each year that are unable to find a mate. This is also an area of debate, for, while some studies have found little evidence for the presence of such 'floaters' after territory establishment (Webber 1975), some males in Wytham are found breeding in their second year but were not identified as doing so in their first. Although in any one year it is not possible to catch and identify every male in the breeding population, the number that are missed is insufficient to account for this observation (Clobert *et al.* 1988). It follows then, that, either these birds held territory outside the study population, or they bred in the wood but nested in a natural hole, or they indeed failed to breed.

Effects of weather

In our northern latitudes, it is natural to believe that the winter must be the hardest time for the birds and certainly, if natural foods such as beechmast are scarce, this may be true. From the results of the BTO Garden Birds Feeding Survey, O'Connor (1980) found that winters in which large numbers of Great Tits visited garden feeders were associated with a subsequent drop in the breeding population. This is because the birds were more likely to come into gardens when natural food stocks were low, and, as we have seen, this is associated with a decline in breeding density between years (Riddington 1992). We have seen that food, population density and social dominance all have a bearing on the survival of Great Tits, but what of winter weather? How do these little birds cope in harsh conditions?

The weather can affect birds in two ways. One is the direct influence of exposure to low temperature or rainfall. The other is an indirect effect. Hard weather increases the bird's food requirements but may also reduce the availability or accessibility of food. For example, it does not matter much how good the Beech crop is if it is hidden under 30 cm of snow. While the winter temperature in Finland may influence strongly the changes in density in those northern populations (Von Haartman 1973), its influence in the milder British climate is very much weaker and operates in a way that suggests an indirect rather than a direct effect on the birds (Clobert *et al.* 1987, 1988). One reason is that the birds make use of behavioural and physiological adaptations that buffer them against the weather. These might be so obvious that, at first sight, the bird's actions do not even appear to be adaptive. For example, Great Tits prefer to roost overnight in a secure shelter such as a tree hole, and only if these are in short supply will they roost in the open. Drent (1987) found that birds roosting in open sites were more likely to die of exposure or predation by owls than birds roosting in nestboxes, so this behaviour is adaptive. A result is that competition for roost sites may be intense, and in part can account for the poorer survival rate of females since they more often lose in competition with males. A further behavioural adaptation, and one that we have already seen, is the formation of winter flocks. Another is that, as the temperature drops, the tits increase their amount of body fat as insurance against poor feeding conditions. Since they reduce their fat reserves when conditions improve again, it is clear that this must be a deliberate strategy (Haftorn 1976; Lehikoinen 1986; Gosler 1987b). Finally, Reinertsen and Haftorn (1986) found that in Norway, when the night was very cold and especially if food was short, Great Tits lowered their body temperature to reduce energy expenditure; the scale of this hypothermia depended on the air temperature. In this way, some individuals lowered their body temperature from the normal 41.8 °C to the remarkably low value of 32 °C with a consequent energy saving of 15–20 per cent. If food was abundant, however, the tits maintained their body temperature closer to 40 °C, irrespective of the air temperature.

In considering these adaptations, I have returned to the issues with which this chapter opened. Chapter 12 considers the other prerequisite for evolution, namely that the characteristics concerned are inherited genetically.

12

NATURE OR NURTURE

EVOLUTION by natural selection results in the great diversity of adaptations that we see in nature, and we have seen many examples of these in the Great Tit. In Chapter 11 we saw that adaptations develop over time from the fact that individuals with different characteristics are more or less likely to survive as a result of those characteristics. Evolution can be said to have occurred, however, only if, as a result of that differential survival, there is a change in the constitution of the gene pool of the population in subsequent generations (Chapter 4). This can occur only if the traits responsible for the differences in survival are inherited genetically from the parents, rather than being due to differences in environment. Such traits are said to be heritable. In this book we have often seen that the Great Tit's biology affords us almost unparalleled opportunities for detailed enquiry which might be impossible to pursue in relation to other species. For this reason there has been a growing interest in the last ten to fifteen years in the genetics of Great Tit populations and in the role of heritability in the evolution of adaptive traits. In this brief chapter, I shall describe some of the results of this research and introduce the principal techniques used by ornithologists to identify which traits are indeed heritable.

Why is genetic inheritance necessary for evolution? To answer this, let us take an apparently simple trait such as body size (the Great Tit is fully grown at fledging). Now, suppose that the variation in body size has no genetic component: in other words, that large Great Tits are large simply because they were fed more by their parents when they were nestlings. Let us now assume that in the year in which these birds fledge environmental conditions dictate that only the larger youngsters survive to breed in the following year. Although on average the survivors may comprise the largest of their year, they do not carry genes for large size as they were large only because they had been fed well. Hence, their own chicks will show a range of sizes that is due only to the quantity of food that they in turn receive. All that selection for large birds has made absolutely no difference to the genetic constitution of the population, and consequently the next generation is no better adapted to its circumstances, which may again favour larger body size. Following such a system, the average size of Great Tits in the population may change from generation to generation simply because of differences in the abundance of caterpillars during the breeding season. If it had been genetically determined, however, selection for larger size should have resulted in a shift in the subsequent composition of the population's gene pool, with the result that a greater proportion of their young (the grandchildren of our starting generation) would have been large-bodied. As a result, they would be better adapted if the environment still favoured larger body size, and a greater proportion of them might survive than of their parent's generation. Evolution would then have occurred. In fact, body size in the Great Tit is highly heritable. About half of the variation in body size observed between individuals can be attributed to heritable genetic variation.

The simple picture that I have painted here raises many questions. Where does the variation come from upon which natural selection operates? Why, if selection always favours large young, do Great Tits not get bigger and bigger with each succeeding generation? And why does selection not gradually whittle away at that genetic variation until there is none left and all Great Tits are the same, ideal, large size? The answers to these questions (where known) are complex and are largely beyond the scope of this book because they are problems which still puzzle evolutionary biologists generally, but, even here, work on the Great Tit can help us to understand what is going on. With regard to the first question, the origin of the genetic variation upon which selection acts in any organism is random mutations in the genetic material (the genome) that occur during cell division. Since this means that new variation is constantly being generated, it gives a partial reason why, in large populations, selection does not result in the complete loss of genetic variation. This is a general biological phenomenon that we need not pursue further, but we should consider the other questions. The reason why Great Tits are not constantly increasing in size with each successive generation is partly that selection does *not* always favour large birds. Although, under certain circumstances, larger young may have an advantage through being socially dominant, they are more expensive for the parents to produce as they require more food. Hence there will always be forces operating in favour of smaller birds. When the population density is low and competition less intense, proportionately more smaller birds survive to breed, so that in successive generations the strength and even direction of selection (for larger or smaller young) may change. In some populations, there is actually evidence for a reduction in body size following a decline in the intensity of competition for nest sites (Dhondt *et al.* 1979). Natural selection itself may therefore be density-dependent.

There is, however, another reason why body size is not constantly increasing, and one that I have already touched upon. In previous chapters, I described how the female balances or 'trades off' the size of chicks against their number, and how the decisions involved were related partly to the density of the population. Thus, in a year of high population density, more pairs raise smaller broods, which results in the production of larger young. These young are larger, however, because they received more food (as the parents' efforts were shared between fewer chicks) and not because they carried genes for larger size. So, although there are indeed genes for body size, the density-dependent selection that acts on the juvenile population through competition actually operates on variation that has been generated by environmental rather than genetic factors (Perrins 1988). It should be mentioned also that, although competition between males may favour larger birds, there is no evidence that this is true for females. This could be because most females are subordinate to males, and the effect of this is greater than any effect of competition between the females themselves. Furthermore, small females are often able to breed earlier than larger ones, because they require less food. Since earlier nests produce more recruits (Chapter 11), this must in turn select a little in favour of smaller females. Because half of the genes for body size (in sons as well as daughters) are inherited from the mother, the lack of selection for large size in females (or indeed active selection against large size in females) must result in a reservoir of genetic variation for smaller size within the female half of the population, which reduces the loss of genetic variation.

A Great Tit chick receives a feed. The degree to which genes for body size are expressed when the bird is full-grown depends on good nutrition when in the nest.

We may ask how it is possible for a trait such as body size to be under genetic control and yet for selection not to influence the gene pool. The reason is that, while an individual may carry genes for a particular body size, there is a great deal of growing that needs to be done after hatching to achieve this. Van Noordwijk (1988) and Henrich (1989) found that the growth rate of Great Tit chicks was determined purely by the environmental conditions of the brood. This in turn means that, if food is not limiting, the chicks will grow until they reach the size determined by their genes. If food is short, however, they may be prevented from reaching that genetically determined value. Van Noordwijk (1987) pointed out that our ability to estimate the heritability of a trait such as body size depends on the quality of the environment to allow expression of the genes that the chicks carry. Intimately tied up with our understanding of the inheritance of such traits is the method used to estimate heritability.

Because of the complexity of the genetics of ecologically important traits such as body size or clutch size, we cannot look directly at the genes present in a population. Instead, we have to infer inheritance from the degree of similarity between close relatives such as parents and offspring or full siblings. Having measured a trait such as body size (by measuring weight or tarsus length) in birds whose relationship we think we know (parents and offspring, for example), statistical methods (such as linear regression) can be used to estimate what proportion of the variation in tarsus length of the chicks is likely to be due to inheritance from the parents. While these methods are actually rather simple to apply, interpreting the results is fraught with difficulty. The main problem is known as the 'common-environment' problem. In the case of body size, all that we can actually measure is the degree of similarity between parents and offspring. Let us again suppose that body size has no genetic basis, but that for social reasons larger parents obtain better territories and are therefore better able to feed their brood. They are therefore likely to produce larger chicks. In such a situation, parents and offspring are similar in size, but there is no genetic involvement.

This is exactly analogous to the human case of social class and inherited wealth. Across the whole human population of Britain the wealth of fathers and sons is correlated but there is no gene for the size of one's bank account. Unlike the case with bank accounts, however, there is a way around this problem that we can use to study heritability in the birds. We have seen that chicks can be moved at an early age between nests with no detrimental effect to parents or young. So if we swap broods in this way, allow the chicks to be raised by foster parents and then measure them, if they still resemble their real genetic parents more than their foster parents we can more reasonably assume that the similarity is due to shared genes rather than to a shared or common environment. Sabine Henrich carried out such manipulations in a wood near Basel in Switzerland. However, she also altered the brood size of some nests by a third, so that some parents were raising larger and some smaller broods than the size of clutch that they had laid; raising an enlarged brood was considered to be equivalent to breeding under poor conditions where food was limiting, while a reduced brood was equivalent to good breeding conditions. These experiments showed that under good conditions the heritability of body size was about 40 per cent, i.e., chicks resembled their real parents; but, if the foster parents were stressed by being given a large brood, the chicks fledged at a lower weight and there was no resemblance between them and the real parents, but they did grow up to show a similarity in size to their foster parents. Hence, larger parents are likely to raise larger young for environmental reasons when under stress, while when food is abundant they may raise larger young because they carry genes for larger size which are inherited by, and expressed in, their offspring (Henrich 1989).

By comparing parents and offspring, several traits of ecological importance in the Great Tit have been shown to have a genetic basis. These include both tarsus (Garnett 1981; Henrich 1989) and bill lengths (Gosler 1987a), adult and fledgling weight, egg size, date of laying, and clutch size (see Van Noordwijk 1987 for a review). In most of these traits, between a quarter and three-quarters of the observed variation among individuals can be attributed to genetic variation between them. Given its ecological significance, clutch size is a particularly interesting case in which the effect of genes (nature) and environment (nurture) are especially difficult to disentangle. There are two main lines of evidence that clutch size is heritable. First, mothers and daughters tend to lay clutches of similar size relative to the average clutch size of the year in which they laid. In other words, if a female lays a comparatively large clutch in one year, it is likely that a daughter hatching from one of those eggs will also lay a comparatively large clutch when she comes to breed. Second, individual females tend to lay clutches of similar size in different years, in different territories and with different males. Indeed, there is no similarity in the clutch sizes of different females breeding in different years but in the same territory and with the same male (Van Noordwijk *et al.* 1981). This apparent lack of an environmental effect on clutch size is curious, since it will be recalled that Perrins (1991) found a strong relationship between the caterpillar density and the clutch size. That relationship, however, was found across the averages of different years: years of high caterpillar density were years of large average clutch size and vice versa. The analyses carried out by Van Noordwijk, on the other hand, effectively ignored the variation in clutch size that existed between years because he looked only at the relative clutch size that a female laid (relative to the average clutch size for the year). The different conclusions of these two studies suggest that the differences in caterpillar density that occur between years are greater than the differences in caterpillar density that exist between territories of birds breeding in the same year. This is because the variation in caterpillar numbers between territories is insufficient to influence clutch size, but the differences between years are sufficiently great to have an effect.

Recently, Sacha Haywood has shown that there is yet another environmental source of variation in clutch size. By analysing the data for clutch size recorded over many years at Wytham, and taking into account the size, date and year of the clutch from which mothers had hatched themselves, he was able to show that a female fledgling's weight had an effect on the size of clutch that she subsequently laid if she survived to breed (Haywood and Perrins 1992). While this suggests that the environment of a chick during growth and development can affect aspects of its future breeding performance, it is not at all clear how such a mechanism might work.

This chapter has shown that the characteristics of the birds that we watch are the result of a complex interplay of many factors, both genetic and environmental. The most significant cause of variation in the Great Tit's environment today is man. The next and final chapter explores in more detail the relationship that we have with the Great Tit.

13

THE GREAT TIT AND MAN

TO study the biology of a bird today is often to study it in a world so altered by our activities that we can only guess at how our results may relate to the natural order. This is especially true in Europe, where the natural vegetation has persisted as a patchwork remnant for hundreds, or thousands, of years. It would be wrong to think that without man the European environment would be static. Before us, its history was dynamic on every scale. As trees matured, died and fell, they created breaks in the forest cover that allowed the succession of new growth and opportunities for light-demanding plant species and their associated fauna that could not otherwise survive in the forest. As lakes were filled with sediment deposited by their inflowing streams, they provided a rapidly changing succession of habitats from fringing marsh, through wet scrub or carr to woodland, each with its own distinct community of invertebrates and birds. Periodically, the world was plunged into a glacial episode in which vast areas of the northern hemisphere were encased in ice. Hence, the species present at any place and at any time were those that could make a living from the particular set of conditions, and could compete successfully with the other species present and attempting to do likewise. So it is today, but the impact of our own species has been so extensive that the birds that have persisted to the present day in Europe are those able to exploit the peculiar set of environmental conditions that we have created – be they coppiced woodland, lowland heath, arable farmland or suburban garden.

Here man has unwittingly acted as an agent of selection and it is a matter for debate whether this has been 'natural' or not. However one views it, the essential difference between the effects of human and non-human processes is the speed with which changes occur. The change in climate from full interglacial to fully glacial conditions occurred so slowly that birds were able to develop new breeding and wintering ranges and to evolve new migration routes. The change from extensive forest over most of Europe to the agricultural and seminatural landscape of modern times was much more rapid and led to the loss of species from many areas. In Ireland, for example, where the fragmentation and loss of the original hardwood forest has been as extensive as anywhere in Europe, there are no woodpeckers. Other woodland species are also absent from the avifauna. Since the subfossil record indicates that woodpeckers once existed in Ireland, the reduction in forest cover to the situation prevailing in 1800, of widely scattered, small woodland plots and a woodland cover of only 2 per cent, is strongly implicated as the cause of their disappearance (Wilson 1977; Hutchinson 1989).

For many species, the break-up and management of the ancient woodlands was beneficial because it created a more diverse mosaic of habitats, with woodland interspersed with open meadow. The woodland itself, managed by the selective thinning of the major timber or 'standard' trees, and by the rotational coppicing of the underwood, created greater structural diversity than the original 'high' forest, in which such diversity occurred only when a tree fall opened the canopy. To see the structure of that primary forest today we must go to the last remnant – the Bialowieza National Park in eastern Poland. Three features of the Bialowieza forest habitats are striking to the observer who is used to the tamed woodlands of Britain. First, the diversity of tree species within a small area is great. Second, the trees are immensely tall (often 30 m or more) and straight, with barely any side branching for perhaps three-quarters of their height. Third, the shrub layer is sparse or absent except in the area of a recent tree fall. This explains the habit of the mature trees, because only the fastest-growing are able to compete successfully to reach the canopy and there is little point in their putting out side branches into the dark understorey of the wood. The sparsity of the shrub layer means that many bird species that are widespread in managed woodland, where they nest in the coppiced underwood, are restricted in high forest to tree-fall areas, where they nest in the regrowth or on the upended root plate of the fallen tree. This results in a low breeding density for these bird species.

In Chapter 4, we found that Great Tit density also was very low in the Bialowieza forest habitats, with fewer than three pairs per 10 ha (Tomialojc

Primary forest habitat in Bialowieza National Park, Poland. Note the diversity of tree species, the accumulation of dead wood and the sparse understorey of the forest.

Trees such as this Oak, which is over four hundred years old, reach massive sizes in the primary forest of Bialowieza. Note the straightness and lack of side-branching.

et al. 1984). By observing the response of Great Tits to recorded song, however, and thereby mapping the extent of their territories, Tomialojc and his co-workers showed that there was in fact little ground unoccupied by this species, so the low density reflected a very large average territory size. They also found that the low density was unlikely to have resulted from a shortage of nest holes, since they found more than fifty suitable tree cavities per 10 ha in old woodland stands. Instead, they suggested that the low density probably resulted from a high rate of predation by mammals on breeding birds, their eggs and nestlings. This was supported by their estimate that, in most years, some 60 per cent of breeding attempts failed to produce any fledged young. We cannot know how typical is Bialowieza of the original forest cover of Europe: the continental climate of the region is quite different from that of the western seaboard, which is so influenced by the Gulf Stream of the North Atlantic, and there is evidence that the diversity of tree species present today in traditionally managed ancient seminatural woodlands of Britain reflects that of the wildwood from which much of it was derived (Peterken 1981; Rackham 1986). Whether or not we use this remnant forest as a model with which to compare modern woodlands, estimates of breeding-bird density alone suggest that our managed woods offer a more benign environment for the Great Tit than did the wildwood of pre-human times. The high density of birds supported by traditional 'coppice-with-standards' management methods, however, compensates only a little for the loss of the vast expanse of forest that once blanketed western Europe.

More rapid and devastating in its effect on bird populations than forest clearance is the fragmentation of seminatural areas in the twentieth century. This has resulted from the construction of barriers such as major trunk roads, impeding the free movement of birds and other animals between areas of suitable habitat. Small woodlands can support only small populations, and these are more at risk of local extinction through the action of chance events such as poor breeding success. If immigration to those woods is obstructed by physical barriers or by the lack of proximity to a population source, recolonization becomes increasingly unlikely, so that the diversity of species in those woods will gradually decline. In this book, I have suggested that the success of the Great Tit in the modern world stems partly from its adaptability, but even this species provides us with evidence for these effects of habitat fragmentation. In Chapter 4 we saw that small woodlands in the Frankfurt area of Germany were unable to support viable populations of the Great Tit without immigration (Bäumer-März and Schmidt 1985). Small woods are also less likely than large ones to provide the diversity of resources required by the tits throughout the year: namely, insect food for the breeding season and tree seed such as beechmast when those insect stocks become low in winter. So, once again, the opportunity for the birds to move between sites is essential for the continuation of the local population.

Our attack on the forest cover of Europe has, in recent years, included elements that are more subtle than the direct action of deforestation. 'Acid precipitation' resulting from the release into the atmosphere of industrial pollutants such as sulphur dioxide, now threatens large areas of woodland in Europe. The effects of this on woodland birds such as the Great Tit are now becoming apparent. Drent and Woldendorp (1989) studied these effects in the Buunderkamp forest in the Netherlands. The Netherlands suffers the highest rate of forest decline caused by acid precipitation in Europe, and the Buunderkamp is an area of mixed and conifer plantation situated on poor sandy soils, which have a naturally low pH anyway; these factors have combined to exacerbate the situation there. The authors describe the chemical effects of acidification on various parts of the ecosystem, but especially on the availability to the birds of calcium for eggshell formation. Between 1986 and 1988, more than half of the Great Tit females studied laid one or more thin-shelled eggs in the clutch, and some of their eggs had no shell at all. The authors also noted that the incidence of such deformities had increased in recent years, suggesting that these effects were not the result solely of the soil pH, although the symptoms did not occur in woodlands on clay and loam soils. Other resident birds (other tits, Nuthatch and Great Spotted Woodpecker) also showed irregularities in their eggs, although migrant species, such as the Pied Flycatcher, did not.

The effects described by Drent and Woldendorp of acidification on birds clearly result from some effect of acidification on the birds' food supply, such as a reduction in the abundance of snails, but we should, also consider the effect of forest damage on the main food supply of the tits during the breeding season – caterpillars. In the long term it is obvious that forest die-back results in a loss of habitat, since dead trees do not support defoliating insects, but, in the short term the interactions are more complex. The response of trees under stress (such as low pH) depends on the nature and intensity of stress imposed. Speight and Wainhouse (1989) describe how low levels of stress result in an increased production of the secondary chemicals (such as tannins) that protect the tree against insect attack. This production occurs at the expense of growth production. Greater stresses, however, can result in a reduction in the production of these chemicals and in an increase in the concentration of nutrients such as protein in the leaves. This can greatly enhance their suitability for such insects as aphids. Van Noordwijk (1990) suggested that, if this enhancement affected cater-pillars also, in the short term local stress in trees could increase the food supply for birds. This is of course a small consolation when one considers that a flush of insects on a tree in one year, which is beneficial to the birds, may represent that tree's last gasp and that it may be dead a few years later. It does, however, serve well to illustrate yet again the complexity of the interactions that can be involved in what, on the face of it, is a simple system (caterpillar eats leaf, Great Tit eats caterpillar).

Man's impact on the Great Tit has sometimes affected unexpected aspects of its biology. Bergman (1980) described how, before 1950, more than 80 per cent of male Great Tits in Finland and Sweden sang song types with three notes in each phrase ('tea-tea-cher, tea-tea-cher' rather than 'tea-cher, tea-cher'). Since then, however, the incidence of 'conventional' two-note songs had increased so that by 1980 fewer than 10 per cent were singing three-note songs in the towns and such singers had become scarcer in rural areas also. Bergman suggested that this occurred because of an increasingly noisy environment in which only two out of the three notes were likely to be heard. The increase in the use of the two-note pattern thus represented an evolved loss of redundancy in the birds' songs. Since three-note songs would have suffered from the same problem in windy areas, this may explain why they had never been noted as the predominant song type further west in Europe, where song had been extensively studied.

So far in this chapter, I have painted a rather pessimistic picture of our relationship with the Great Tit, but there have been many instances in this book which show that the birds are not always on a losing side. I have suggested above that traditional methods of woodland management may favour the species, and we have already seen evidence that the provision of nestboxes in woods with a shortage of natural holes can increase the density of breeding pairs that can be supported. Nestboxes are often more likely to provide a more appropriate size of cavity in which to nest than are natural holes. Furthermore, birds that use certain kinds of nestbox (p. 46) are less vulnerable to attack from predators than are the birds that use natural holes. Probably the most significant benefit that the birds receive from humanity, however, is the provision of food at garden birdtables and feeders, and especially when natural food is scarce in late summer and winter. Although breeding success is usually poorer in garden sites than in woods, because of the former's comparatively poor insect density, food provided in gardens in winter may make a substantial difference to the survival chances of woodland birds. We have seen (Chapter 11) that the number of Great Tits visiting garden feeders in winter increases when the natural woodland food supply (especially beechmast) is poor.

Clearly, then, the birds leave the woods when conditions there become too harsh, but just how much of a difference does garden feeding really make in winter? Cowie and Hinsley (1988) and Riddington (1992) investigated this by questioning householders in Cardiff (287 households) and west Oxford (253) respectively about how much food they provided for the birds in winter. In both cases, about 70–75 per cent of households provided food in winter but 35–40 per cent in summer. In Cardiff, 41 per cent of households provided peanuts for tits, while 62 per cent did so in Oxford. Cowie and Hinsley also found that feeders were visited with especially high frequency by female and juvenile Great Tits in August and September. This again must be related to a shortage of natural food at that time.

The garden environment is not entirely benign for small birds. Cowie and Hinsley found that, on average, one in four households in their survey

---

A major new road slices through relict ancient semi-natural woodland. The loss of woodland itself is not the only damage caused by such developments in Europe, for, by reducing the free passage of individuals, habitat fragmentation can reduce the viability of bird populations (such as the Great Tit's) persisting in the small woods that result.

Urban sprawl usually results in a net loss of habitat for woodland birds such as the Great Tit. Where broad-leaved woodland abuts onto suburban gardens, as in east Oxford, however, it need not always be so, as food provided at feeders can provide a vital life-line in winter for tits forced out of the woods by food shortage.

owned a cat and that this was the same as a national average figure reported elsewhere. Since it is known that each cat kills an average of at least five birds each year, they point out that this is a significant rate of loss. The important question to ask, however, is whether the survival rates of birds visiting gardens are sufficiently enhanced by the provision of extra food for the populations to sustain this level of predation. Riddington (1992) addressed this by comparing the subsequent survival rate of Great Tits that visited gardens near Wytham with that of birds that visited feeders within the wood. He found no difference in their apparent survival rates. Since birds that wintered outside Wytham were less likely to obtain a territory inside the wood than those that remained in the wood for the winter, the likelihood of his finding them subsequently, however, must have been much lower. He concluded therefore that the survival over winter of the garden visitors must have been much greater than that of the birds that remained in the wood. Hence, there are both costs and benefits to the birds if they leave the wood to feed in winter. The benefits are clear if they are more likely to survive the winter, but the longer-term costs may also be considerable if they are prevented subsequently from entering the best habitats to breed.

I have repeatedly presented examples in this book of how the Great Tit offers opportunities for the research biologist. In the past this was largely because they were common and accessible: they used nestboxes to breed and peanuts to feed. In short, they were convenient. The great store of information accumulated in the literature on this bird means, however, that the Great Tit, and species like it, now offer unprecedented opportunities to examine and measure the damage that mankind is inflicting on the natural environment of Europe. We have learned much about the Great Tit. We now need to apply this knowledge urgently to understand its relationship with us, so that we may inflict less damage in the future.

Bibliography

Baker, M.C., *American Naturalist* 112 (1978) 779–81

Baker, M.C., McGregor, P.K., and Krebs, J.R., *Ornis Scandinavica* 18 (1987) 186–8

Barba, E., and Gil-Delgado, J.A., *Ornis Scandinavica* 21 (1990) 296–8

Barba, E., Gil-Delgado, J.A., and Lopez, G., *Mediterránea* 10 (1988) 5–11; *Ardeola* 36 (1989) 83–7

Bäumer-März, C., and Schmidt, K-H., *Die Vogelwarte* 33 (1985) 1–7

Bengtsson, H., and Rydén, O., *Behavioural Ecology and Sociobiology* 12 (1983) 243–51

Bergman, G., *Ornis Fennica* 57 (1980) 97–111

Berndt, R., and Henß, M., *Die Vogelwarte* 24 (1967) 17–37

Berressem, K.G., Berressem, H., and Schmidt, K-H., *Journal für Ornithologie* 124 (1983) 431–45

Berthold, P., *Ardea* 64 (1976) 140–54

Betts, M.M., *Journal of Animal Ecology* 24 (1955) 282–323

Björklund, M., Møller, A.P., Sundberg, J., and Westman, B., *Animal Behaviour* 43 (1992) 691–3

Björklund, M., and Westman B., *Ornis Scandinavica* 17 (1986) 99–105

Björklund, M., Westman, B., and Allander, K., *Behaviour* 11 (1989) 257–69

Blondel, J., Clamens, A., Cramm, P., Gaubert, H., and Isenmann, P., *Ardea* 75 (1987) 21–34

Boer-Hazewinkel, J. Den., *Ardea* 75 (1987) 99–110

Bösenberg, K., *Beiträge zur Vogelkunde* 9 (1964) 249–62

Brian, A.D., *Scottish Naturalist* 61 (1949) 144–55

Brown, J.L., *American Naturalist* 103 (1969) 347–54

Bulmer, M.G., *Heredity* 30 (1973) 313–25

Cairns, J., *Journal of the Bombay Natural History Society* 53 (1956) 367–73

Ceballos, P., *Real Academia de Ciencias Madrid* 25 (1972) 1–61

Charnov, R., *Theoretical Population Biology* 9 (1976) 129–36

Clobert, J. Lebreton, J.D., and Allaine, D., *Ardea* 75 (1987) 133–42

Clobert, J., Perrins, C.M., McCleery, R.H., and Gosler, A.G., *Journal of Animal Ecology* 57 (1988) 287–306

Cowie, R.J., *Nature* 268 (1977) 137–9

Cowie, R.J., and Hinsley, S.A., *Ardea* 75 (1987) 81–90; *Bird Study* 35 (1988) 163–8

Curio, E., *Verhandlungen der Deutschen Zoologischen Gesellschaft* 1979 (1979), 221; *Ardea* 75 (1987) 35–42

Curio, E., Klump, G., and Regelmann, K., *Oecologia* 60 (1983) 83–8

Czaja-Topiñska, J., *Acta Ornithologica* 11 (1969) 357–76

Davies, N.B., *Ibis* 120 (1978) 509–14

Delacour, J., and Vaurie, C., *Oiseau* 20 (1950) 91–121

Dhondt, A.A., [1970a] 'De regulatie der aantallen in Gentse Koolmeespopulaties, *Parus major* L.' (University of Ghent Ph.D. thesis, 1970); [1970b] *Bird Study* 17 (1970), 282–6; [1971a] *Le Gerfaut* 61, (1971), 125–35; [1971b] *Proceedings of the Advanced Study Institute on 'Dynamics of numbers in Populations',* (Oosterbeek 1970) (1971), 532–47; *Le Gerfaut* 63, (1973) 187–209; *Oecologia* 42 (1979) 139–57; *American Naturalist* 129 (1987) 213–20

Dhondt, A.A., Adriaensen, F., Matthysen, E., and Kempenaers, B., *Nature* 348 (1990) 723–5

Dhondt, A.A., Eyckerman, R., and Hublé, J., *Biological Journal of the Linnean Society* 11 (1979) 289–94

Dhondt, A.A., and Hublé, J., [1968a] *Angewandt Ornithologie* 3 (1968) 20–24; [1968b] *Bird Study* 15, (1968) 127–34

Dhondt, A.A., and Schillemans, J., *Animal Behaviour* 31 (1983) 902–12

Dolnik, V.R., and Gavrilov, V.M., *Auk* 96 (1979) 253–64

Drent, P.J., 'The functional ethology of territoriality in the Great Tit *Parus major* L.'

(University of Groningen Ph.D. thesis, 1983); *Ardea* 72. (1984) 127–62; *Ardea* 75 (1987) 59–72

Drent, P.J., and Woldendorp, J.W., *Nature* 339 (1989) 431

Dunn, E.K., *Journal of Animal Ecology* 46 (1977) 633–52

Duyck, J., and Duyck, J., *Wielewaal* 50 (1984) 416

East, M., and Perrins, C.M., *Ibis* 130 (1988) 393–401

Eguchi, K., *Researches on Population Ecology* 22 (1980) 284–300

Einloft-Achenbach, H., and Schmidt, K-H., *Die Vogelwarte* 32 (1984) 161–82

Ennion, E.A.R., *British Birds* 55 (1962) 187–8

Erichsen, J.T., Krebs, J.R., and Houston, A.I., *Journal of Animal Ecology* 49 (1980) 271–6

Eyckerman, R., *Die Giervalk* 64 (1974) 29–40

Feeny, P.P., *Ecology* 51 (1970) 565–81

Flegg, J.J.M., and Cox, C.J., *Bird Study* 16 (1969) 147–57

Fretwell, S.D., *Populations in a Seasonal Environment*, Princeton University Press, Princeton, 1972

Garnett, M.C., 'Some aspects of body size in the Great Tit' (University of Oxford D.Phil. thesis, 1976); *Ibis* 123 (1981) 31–41

Geer, T.A., *Ibis* 124 (1982) 159–67

Gibb, J.A., *Ibis* 92 (1950), 507–39; [1954a] *Ibis* 96 (1954), 513–43; [1954b] *Bird Study* 1 (1954), 40–48; *Bird Study* 4 (1957), 207–15; *Bird Banding* 41 (1970), 40-41

Gibb, J.A., and Betts, M.M., *Journal of Animal Ecology* 32 (1963), 489–533

Gil-Delgado, J.A., and Barba, E., *Mediterránea* 9 (1987), 29–40

Ginn, H.B., and Melville, D.S., *Moult in Birds*, BTO, Tring, 1983

Gompertz, T., *British Birds* 54 (1961), 369–418; *Beihefte der Vogelwelt* 1 (1968), 63–92

Gosler, A.G. in Lack, P.C. (ed.), *The Atlas of Wintering Birds in Britain and Ireland*, T. and A.D. Poyser, Calton, 1986, p. 354; [1987a] *Ibis* 129 (1987) 451–76; [1987b] 'Some aspects of bill morphology in relation to ecology in the Great Tit *Parus major*' (University of Oxford D.Phil. thesis, 1987); [1987c] *Ardea* 75 (1987)

91–8; *Acta XX Congressus Internationalis Ornithologici* (Supplement) 361 (1990); *Bird Study* 38 (1991) 1–9; in Cramp, S., and Perrins, C.M. (eds), *The Birds of the Western Palearctic* Vol VII, OUP, Oxford, 1993, pp. 259–65

Greenwood, P.J., Harvey, P.H., and Perrins, C.M., *Nature* 271 (1978) 52–4; [1979a] *Ornis Fennica* 56 (1979) 75–86; [1979b] *Journal of Animal Ecology* 48 (1979) 123–42

Grubb, T.C., *Animal Behaviour* 35 (1987) 794–806

Guildford, T., and Dawkins, M., *Animal Behaviour* 35 (1987) 1838–45

Haftorn, S., *Fauna* 4 (1950) 121–39; *Norwegian Journal of Zoology* 4 (1976) 241–71; [1981a] *Ornis Scandinavica* 12 (1981) 169–85; [1981b] *Cinclus* 4 (1981) 9–26; *Cinclus* 6 (1983) 22–38

Hailman, J., *Wilson Bulletin* 101 (1989) 305–43

Hartley, P.H.T., *Journal of Animal Ecology* 22 (1953) 261–88

Haywood, S., and Perrins, C.M., *Proceedings of the Royal Society, London, Series B* 249 (1992) 195–7

Henrich, S.G., 'The genetical ecology of nestling growth in the Great Tit *Parus major* L.' (University of Basel Ph.D. thesis, 1989)

Hildén, O., *Ornis Fennica* 55 (1978) 120–25

Hinde, R.A., *Behaviour* (Supplement) 2 (1952) 1–201

Houston, A.I., Krebs, J.R., and Erichsen, J.T., *Behavioural Ecology and Sociobiology* 6 (1980) 169–75

Hunter, M.L., and Krebs, J.R., *Journal of Animal Ecology* 48 (1979) 759–85

Hutchinson, C.D., *Birds in Ireland*, T. and A.D. Poyser, Calton, 1989

Järvi, T., and Bakken, M., *Animal Behaviour* 32 (1984) 590–96

Järvi, T., Walso, O., and Bakken, M., *Ethology* 76 (1987) 334–42

Jones, P.J., 'Some aspects of the feeding ecology of the Great Tit *Parus major*' (University of Oxford D.Phil. thesis, 1973)

Källander, H., *Ibis* 116 (1974) 365–7; *Ornis Scandinavica* 12 (1981) 244–8; *Vår Fågelvärld* 42 (1983) 413–24

Keil, W., *Angewandte Ornithologie* 1 (1963) 141–8

Kiziroglu, I., *Anzeiger Schudlingskde Pflanzenschutz Umweltschutz* 55 (1982) 170–74

Kluijver, H.N., *Ardea* 38 (1950) 99–135; *Ibid.* 39 (1951) 1–135; *Proceedings of the Advanced Study Institute on 'Dynamics of numbers in Populations'* (Oosterbeek 1970) (1971) 507–23

Kluijver, H.N., and Tinbergen, L., *Archives Néerlandaises de Zoologie* 10 (1953) 265–89

Krebs, J.R., *Journal of Zoology, London* 162 (1970) 317–33; *Ecology* 52 (1971) 2–22; *Canadian Journal of Zoology* 51 (1973) 1275–88; *Behavioural Ecology and Sociobiology* 1 (1976) 215–27; [1977a] in Stonehouse, B., and Perrins, C.M. (eds.), *Evolutionary Ecology*, Macmillan, London,. 1977, pp. 47–62; [1977b] *Animal Behaviour* 25, 1977), 475–8; *Behavioural Ecology and Sociobiology* 11 (1982) 185–95

Krebs, J.R., Ashcroft, R., and Webber, M.I., *Nature* 271 (1978) 539–42

Krebs, J.R., Ashcroft, R., and Van Orsdol, K., *Animal Behaviour* 29 (1981) 918–23

Krebs, J.R., Avery, M., and Cowie, R.J., *Animal Behaviour* 29 (1981) 635–7

Krebs, J.R., Erichsen, J.T., and Webber, M.I., *Animal Behaviour* 25 (1977) 30–38

Krebs, J.R., Kacelnik, A., and Taylor, P., *Nature* 275 (1978) 27–31

Krebs, J.R., MacRoberts, M.H., and Cullen, J.M., *Ibis* 114 (1972) 507–30

Lack, D., *Natural Regulation of Animal Numbers*, Clarendon Press, Oxford, 1954; *Population Studies of Birds*, Clarendon Press, Oxford, 1966

Laet, J. de, *Ornis Scandinavica* 15 (1984) 73–8; [1985a] *Ibis* 127 (1985) 372–7; [1985b] in Sibley, R.M., and Smith, R.H. (eds.), *Behavioural Ecology*, Blackwell, Oxford, 1985, pp. 375–80

Lambrechts, M. in McGregor, P.K. (ed.), *Playback and Studies of Animal Communication*, Plenum Press, New York, 1992, pp. 135–52

Lambrechts, M., and Dhondt, A.A., *Behavioural Ecology and Sociobiology* 19 (1986) 57–63; *Ardea* 75 (1987) 43–52; [1988a] *Animal Behaviour* 36 (1988) 596–601; [1988b] *Animal Behaviour* 36 (1988) 327–34

Lebreton, J.D. in Blondel, J., Gosler, A.G., Lebreton, J.D., and McCleery, R.H. (eds),

Population Biology of Passerine Birds: An Integrated Approach, Springer, Berlin, 1990, pp. 89–102

Lehikoinen, E., *Ornis Fennica* 63 (1986) 112–19

Lemel, J., *Ornis Scandinavica* 20 [1989a] 226–33; *The Auk* 106 [1989b] 490–92

Lindén, M., *Oikos* 51 (1988) 285–90; 'Reproductive investment and its fitness consequences in the Great Tit *Parus major*' (University of Uppsala Ph.D. thesis, 1990)

Löhrl, H., *Journal für Ornithologie* 114 (1973) 339–47; *Ibid.* 121 (1980) 403–405; *Ibid.* 127 (1986) 51–9

McCleery, R.H., and Clobert, J. in Blondel, J., Gosler, A.G., Lebreton, J.D., and McCleery, R.H., (eds), *Population Biology of Passerine Birds: An Integrated Approach*, Springer, Berlin, 1990, pp. 423–40

McCleery, R.H., and Perrins, C.M. in Sibley, R.M., and Smith, R.H. (eds), *Behavioural Ecology*, Blackwell, Oxford, 1985, pp. 353–73; in Clutton-Brock, T.H. (ed.), *Reproductive Success*, Chicago University Press, Chicago, 1988, pp. 136–53; in Newton, I. (ed.), *Lifetime Reproduction in Birds*, Academic Press, London, 1989, pp. 35–53; in Perrins, C.M., Lebreton, J.D., and Hirons, G.J.M. (eds), *Bird Population Studies – Relevance to Conservation and Management*, OUP, Oxford, 1991, pp. 129–47

Mace, R., *Animal Behaviour* 34 (1986) 621–2; [1987a] *Ardea* 75 (1987) 123–32; [1987b] *Nature* 330 (1987) 745–6

McGregor, P.K., and Avery, M.I., *Behavioural Ecology and Sociobiology* 18 (1986) 311–16

McGregor, P.K., and Horn, A.G., *Animal Behaviour* 43 (1992) 667–76

McGregor, P.K., and Krebs, J.R., [1982a] *Nature* 297 (1982) 60–61; [1982b] *Behaviour* 79 (1982) 126–52; *Behavioural Ecology and Sociobiology* 16 (1984) 49-56; *Behaviour* 86 (1989) 139–59

McGregor, P.K., Krebs, J.R., and Perrins, C.M., *American Naturalist* 118 (1981) 149–59

McGregor, P.K., Krebs, J.R., and Ratcliffe, L.M., *The Auk* 100 (1983) 898–906

Martin, E.W., *Physiological Zoology* 41 (1968) 313–31

Matthysen, E., in Power, D.M. (ed.), *Current Ornithology* 7 (1990) 209–49, Plenum Press, New York

Matthews, J.D., *Forestry* 28 (1955) 107–16

Mertens, J.A.L., *Ardea* 65 (1977) 184–96

Minot, E.O., *Journal of Animal Ecology* 50 (1981) 375–85

Minot, E.O., and Perrins, C.M., *Journal of Animal Ecology* 55 (1986) 331–50

Møller, A.P., *Oikos* 56 (1989) 421–3; *Animal Behaviour* 40 (1990) 1070–79; *Oikos* 63 (1992) 309–11

Morse, D.H., *Ibis* 120 (1978) 298–312

Murphy, M.E., and King, J.R., *Acta XX Congressus Internationalis Ornithologici* (1991) 2186–93

Nager, R. in Blondel, J., Gosler, A.G., Lebreton, J.D., and McCleery, R.H. (eds.), *Population Biology of Passerine Birds: An Integrated Approach*, Springer, Berlin, 1990, pp. 187–97

Newton, I., *Ibis*, 108 (1966) 41–67

Norris, K.J., [1990a] *Behavioural Ecology and Sociobiology* 26 (1990) 129–38; [1990b] *Ibid*. 27 (1990) 275–81

Norris, K.J., and Blakey, J.K., *Ibis* 131 (1989) 436–42

O'Connor, R.J., *Ardea* 68 (1980) 165–83

Oddie, W.J. *Bill Oddie's Little Black Bird Book*, Eyre Methuen, London, 1980

Orell, M., and Ojanen, M., *Ardea* 67 (1979) 130–37; *Ornis Scandinavica* 11 (1980) 43–9; [1983a] *Ardea* 71 (1983) 183–98; [1983b] *Holarctic Ecology* 6 (1983) 413–23

Orions, G., *Some Adaptations of Marsh-nesting Blackbirds*, Princeton University Press, Princeton, 1980

Peterken, G. F., *Woodland Conservation and Management*, Chapman and Hall, London, 1981

Perrins, C.M., 'Some factors influencing brood-size and populations in tits' (University of Oxford D.Phil. thesis, 1963); *Journal of Animal Ecology* 34 (1965) 601–47; *British Birds* 59 (1966) 419–32; *Ibis* 112 (1970) 242–55; *Ibid*. 118 (1976) 580–84; *British Tits*, Collins, London, 1979; *Acta XIX Congressus Internationalis Ornithologici* (1988) 892–9; in Blondel, J., Gosler, A.G., Lebreton, J.D., and McCleery, R.H. (eds.), *Population Biology of Passerine Birds: An Integrated Approach*, Springer,

Berlin, 1990, pp. 121–30 [a], pp. 475–80 [b]; *Ibis* (Supplement) 1 (1991) 49–54

Perrins, C.M., and McCleery, R.H., *Ibis* 127 (1985) 306–15; *Wilson Bulletin* 101 (1989) 236–53

Pettifor, R.A., Perrins, C.M., and McCleery, R.H., *Nature* 336 (1988) 160–62

Pielou, W., 'A life-history study of the Tufted Titmouse, *Parus bicolor* L.' (Michegan State University Ph.D. thesis, 1957)

Pyle, P., Howell, S.N.G., Yunick, R.P., and DeSante, D.F. *Identification Guide to North American Passerines*, Slate Creek Press, California, 1987

Rackham, O., *The History of the Countryside*, J.M. Dent and Sons, London, 1986

Regelmann, K., and Curio., E. *Behavioural Ecology and Sociobiology* 13 (1983) 131–45

Reinertsen, R.E., and Haftorn, S., *Journal of Comparative Physiology* 156 (1986) 655–63

Rheinwald, G., *Bonner Zoologische Beiträge* 32 (1981) 111–26

Riddington, R., 'Some aspects of the dispersal and post-fledging ecology of a population of Great Tits *Parus major*' (University of Oxford D.Phil. thesis, 1992)

Røskaft, E., Järvi, T., Bakken, M., Bech, C., and Reinertsen,. R.E. *Animal Behaviour* 34 (1986) 838–42

Royama, T., *Ibis* 108 (1966) 313–47; *Journal of Animal Ecology* 39 (1970) 619–68

Saitou, T., *Japanese Journal of Ecology* 28 (1978) 199–214; *Journal of the Yamashina Institute of Ornithology* 11 (1979) 137–48 [a]; 149–71 [b]; 172–88 [c]

Sandell, M., and Smith, H.G., *Behavioural Ecology and Sociobiology* 29 (1991) 147–52

Sasvari, L., *Animal Behaviour* 27 (1979) 767–71; *Journal of Applied Ecology* 25 (1988) 807–17; *Animal Behaviour* 43 (1992) 289–96

Schierer, A., *Bulletin de la Societé d'Histoire Naturelle de Colmar* 52 (1965) 29–34

Schifferli, L., *Ibis* 115 (1973) 549–58

Schmidt, K-H., and Wolff, S., *Journal für Ornithologie* 126 (1985) 175–80

Sibley, C.G., and Monroe, B.L., Jr., *Distribution and Taxonomy of the Birds of the World*, Yale University Press, New Haven, 1990

Slagsvold, T., *Journal of Animal Ecology* 53 (1984) 945–53

Slagsvold, T., and Amundsen, T., *Journal of Animal Ecology* 61 (1992) 249–58

Slagsvold, T., and Lifjeld, J.T., *Ecology* 71 (1990) 1258–66

Smal, C.M., and Fairley, J.S., *Holarctic Ecology* 3 (1980) 10–18

Smith, H., Källander, H., and Nilsson, J-Åke, *The Auk* 104 (1987) 700–706; *Journal of Animal Ecology* 58 (1989) 383–401

Smith, J. Maynard, and Harper, D.G.C., *Philosophical Transactions of the Royal Society, London Series B* 319 (1988) 557–70

Smith, J.N.M., and Dawkins, R., *Animal Behaviour* 19 (1971) 695–706

Smith, J.N.M., and Sweatman, H.P.A., *Ecology* 55 (1974) 1216–32

Snow, D.W., 'Systematics and comparative ecology of the genus *Parus* in the Palaearctic region' (University of Oxford D.Phil. thesis, 1953); *Evolution* 8 (1954) 14–28

Speight, M.R., and Wainhouse, D., *Ecology and Management of Forest Insects*, Oxford University Press, Oxford, 1989

Stephens, D.W., and Krebs, J.R., *Foraging Theory*, Princeton University Press, Princeton, 1986

Suhonen, J., and Inki, K., *Animal Behaviour* 44 (1992) 180–81

Székely, T., Szép, T., and Juhász, T., *Oecologia* 78 (1989) 490–95

Thorpe, W., *British Birds* 37 (1943) 29–31

Tinbergen, J.M., *Ardea* 75 (1987) 111–22

Tinbergen, J.M., Balen, J.H. van, Drent, P.J., Cavé, A.J., Mertens, J.A.L., and Boer-Hazewinkel, J. Den., *Netherlands Journal of Zoology* 37 (1987) 180–213

Tinbergen, L., *Archives Néerlandaises de Zoologie* 13 (1960) 265–336

Tomialojc, L., Wesolowski, T., and Walankiewicz, W., *Acta Ornithologica* 29, 1984), 243–310

Ulfstrand, S., *Vår Fågelvärld* (Supplement) 5 (1962) 1–145

Van Balen, J.H., *Ardea* 61 (1973) 1–93; *Ibid.* 68 (1980) 143–64; *Ibid.* 72 (1984) 163–75

Van Balen, J.H., and Cavé, A.J., *Netherlands Journal of Zoology* 20 (1970) 464–74

Van Balen, J.H., Van Noordwijk, A.J., and Visser, J. *Ardea* 75 (1987) 1–11

Van Noordwijk, A.J. in Cooke, F., and Buckley, P.A. (eds.), *Avian Genetics*, Academic Press, London, 1987, pp. 363–80; in De Jong, G. (ed.), *Population Genetics and Evolution*, pp. 124–37, Springer, Berlin, 1988; in Blondel, J., Gosler, A.G., Lebreton, J.D., and McCleery, R.H. (eds), *Population Biology of Passerine Birds: An Integrated Approach*, Springer, Berlin, 1990, pp. 215–22

Van Noordwijk, A.J., Van Balen, J.H., and. Scharloo, W., *Netherlands Journal of Zoology*, 31 (1981) 342–72

Van Noordwijk, A.J., and Scharloo, W., *Evolution* 35 (1981) 674–88

Van Noordwijk, A.J., Van Tienderen, P.H., De Jong, G., and Van Balen, J.H. in Sibley, R., and Smith, R.H. (eds), *Behavioural Ecology*, Blackwell, Oxford, 1985, pp. 381–5

Van Noordwijk, A.J., Scharloo, W., and Van Balen, J.H., *Genetical Research* 51 (1988) 149–62

Van Noordwijk, A.J., and Van Balen, J.H., in Clutton-Brock, T.H. (ed.), *Reproductive Success*, Chicago University Press, 1988, pp. 119–35

Vaurie, C., *The Birds of the Palaearctic Fauna*, H.G. and G. Witherby, London, 1959

Verhulst, S., *Ardea* 80 (1992) 285–92

Vestjens, J.P.M., *De beukenoot als wintervoedsel voor de koolmes* (Parus major) *een vrije keus?*, Institut voor Oecologisch Onderzoek, Arnhem, 1983

Von Haartman, L., *Lintumies* 8 (1973) 7–9

Weary, D.M., Krebs, J.R., Eddyshaw, R., McGregor, P.K., and Horn, A.G., *Animal Behaviour* 36 (1988) 1242–4

Weary, D.M., Lambrechts, M., and Krebs, J.R., *Animal Behaviour* 41 (1991) 540–42

Webber, M.I., 'Some aspects of the non-breeding population dynamics of the Great Tit *Parus major*' (University of Oxford D.Phil. thesis, 1975)

Wilson, J., *Polish Ecological Studies* 3 (1977) 245–56

Wilson, J.D., *Animal Behaviour* 43 (1992) 999–1009

Winkel, W., *Die Vogelwelt* 101 (1980) 30–33

Yavin, S., 'Nest site selection of the Great Tit *Parus major terrae-sanctae*' (University of Tel Aviv M.Sc. thesis, 1987)

Ydenberg, R.C., *Behaviour* 81 (1984) 1–24

Scientific Names

All species mentioned in the text are listed below, with their scientific names.

BIRDS
Goshawk *Accipiter gentilis*
Sparrowhawk *A. nisus*
Pygmy Owl *Glaucidium passerinum*
Great Spotted Woodpecker *Picoides*
  (Dendrocopos) major
larks *Alaudidae*
Swallow *Hirundo rustica*
Blackbird *Turdus merula*
Chiffchaff *Phylloscopus collybita*
Pied Flycatcher *Ficedula hypoleuca*
Long-tailed Tit *Aegithalos caudatus*
Marsh Tit *Parus palustris*
Sombre Tit *P. lugubris*
Willow Tit *P. montanus*
Black-capped Chickadee *P. atricapillus*
Carolina Chickadee *P. carolinensis*
Mexican Chickadee *P. sclateri*
Mountain Chickadee *P. gambeli*
Bridled Titmouse *P. wollweberi*
Siberian Tit *P. cinctus*
Boreal Chickadee *P. hudsonicus*
Chestnut-backed Chickadee *P. rufescens*
Tufted Titmouse *P. bicolor*
Plain Titmouse *P. inornatus*
Crested Tit *P. cristatus*
Coal Tit *P. ater*

Blue Tit *P. caeruleus*
Azure Tit *P. cyanus*
Great Tit *P. major*
Nuthatch *Sitta europaea*
Treecreeper *Certhia familiaris*
sparrows *Passer* spp.
Starling *Sturnus vulgaris*
Chaffinch *Fringilla coelebs*
Bullfinch *Pyrrhula pyrrhula*
buntings *Emberizinae*

TREES
Oak *Quercus robur* and *Q. peraea*
Beech *Fagus sylvatica*
Hazel *Corylus avellana*
Hawthorn *Crataegus* sp.
Yew *Taxus baccata*

MAMMALS
Grey Squirrel *Sciurus Carolensiensis*
Weasel *Mustela nivalis*

INVERTEBRATES
Winter Moth *Operophtera brumata*

Index